Implications for Peace: Montessori Elementary Education

Peggy E. Pate-Smith

Core Faculty: Philip Gang and Marsha Morgan
Field Mentor: Elizabeth Coe

Submitted in Partial Fulfillment for the Degree
Master of Education

Endicott College - TIES Partnership
APA Style

April 7, 2006

Acknowledgements

Implications of Peace: Montessori Elementary Education is an intensive look at many aspects of peace within the Montessori environment and within a teacher in Montessori training. This study would not have been possible without the unwavering support of my husband, William Smith, and my very patient children, Liberty and Seneca Sunshine Smith. I am gratefully indebted to the staff and faculty of Parkview Montessori Magnet School in Jackson, Tennessee for their guidance, encouragement, and support. It is also due to the many dialogues, e-mails and positive energy sent by scores of people who have formed the balcony cheering section for my life that this paper has true meaning.

Abstract

Implications for peace are examined through the Montessori environment and materials. Experiences leading a Montessori teacher into a deeper spiritual awareness and humility in the classroom are disclosed in order to understand the role of the teacher in creating an emotionally safe environment for students. Material created for students to study Nobel Peace Prize Winners, and the ramifications of this study on the greater community of parents and family members, are all explored. Active interviews, reflection, dialogue, and phenomenological research are all utilized in order to develop a greater understanding of peace within the Montessori environment. Peace is also examined through the concepts of inner peace, environmental peace, and peace in relationships.

Table of Contents

Abstract	3
Introduction	5
Chapter 1: Training to be a Montessori Teacher	8
1.1 Active Interview	22
1.2 Nobel Peace Prize Project	27
1.3 Methods	28
1.4 Hermeneutic	31
1.5 Student Interviews	31
1.6 Student Research	36
1.7 Parent Interviews	38
1.8 Wholistic Interpretation	42
1.9 Selective Interpretation	43
1.10 Line by Line Interpretation	45
1.11 Conclusion of Research Project	46
1.12 Brain Gym	48
Chapter 2: Unity throughout the Curriculum	51
2.1 Common Characteristics of a Montessori Classroom	56
2.2 Main Areas of a Montessori Classroom	59
Chapter 3: Exploring the Transformation of a Montessori Teacher	64
3.1 Readings	65
3.2 Influences of Other People	79
3.3 Other Experiences	98
3.4 Perspective Changes	101
3.5 Impacting Others	105
3.6 Themes of Transformation	108
Chapter 4: Program Summary	113
4.1 Inner Peace	114
4.2 Environmental Peace	120
4.3 Peace within Relationships	125
Appendix	132
References	136

Implications for Peace: Montessori Elementary Education

Is it possible that world peace could become more than just a fuzzy concept for politicians and beauty contestants, that it could become, rather, an everyday reality and expectation? Is it feasible that conflict resolution skills are really so simple that a first grader could learn and use them on a daily basis? Are there ways that acting locally can make a difference big enough to make the world a better place?

For the past three years I have been tantalized by these thoughts and questions. These questions started when I was the business owner of a small bookstore. One day I was dusting the shelves when a romance book caught my eye. I normally read non-fiction, but this book seemed to call to me, so I started thumbing through it. The book was a work of historical fiction about a young woman who also owned a bookstore and was an advocate for women's right to vote. That book caused me to start thinking about how many concepts I took for granted, like all genders and races in the U.S. being allowed to vote. These rights came through re-education of what was acceptable and what was not. It then occurred to me, as I looked at the yellow ribbons that hung on my bookstore window representing community members that were separated from their families by war, that perhaps conflict should be approached in the same way that world peace could be achieved through enough people standing up and saying, "Enough. There is a different way to handle conflict, and war is not acceptable and not feasible anymore."

I started asking the people around me, "Do you think world peace is really possible?"

Most of them looked at me as if I were crazy and quickly said, "No." Still, I could not get these thoughts out of my head. It seemed to me that these questions were being put into my heart for a reason that I could not understand, and yet I needed to take them seriously. Shortly after this time I was told that the landlord of my bookstore was selling the building. I made the decision to return to my former occupation as a teacher. What happened next began a journey that I was not expecting but for which I could have nothing but gratitude. This journey led me to the world of Montessori education. It has shifted my view of the world and inspired me to want to share that view with others. It has shown me that peace is a choice, and that transformed adults can create an environment for learning which allows the peace that is naturally within the heart of students the opportunity to blossom.

In January of 2004 I was asked to interview at Parkview Montessori Magnet School for an interim teaching position while a teacher was on maternity leave. When I walked through the doors of this school, my feeling was not what I had expected, judging by the shabby exterior of the building located next to a housing project in one of the poorest sections of town. Warmth, love, and peace would describe my initial feelings when I entered this new world of Montessori education. While the building was just as evidently aged on the inside as the outside, the intangible attitudes of the occupants had transformed it into a place of peace, a place of which I immediately knew I wanted to be a part. As I toured the building I saw students actively engaged in learning and enjoying their day. I did not see students being lined up in tidy rows of desks hunched over workbook pages with a teacher standing in front of the classroom lecturing. Instead, students were quietly working on small individual mats on the floor with many different types of manipulative materials. Teachers were either sitting on the floor with an individual student or sitting on the floor with a small group of students. I found it amazing that even though everyone was doing something different, the rooms were calm and orderly. I had never entered a public, or a private, school that was anything like it. What did Montessori education have to offer that could create such an environment? I was eager to learn more. I felt that perhaps here I could find some answers to the questions I had been asking.

Training to be a Montessori Teacher

After completing my time as an interim teacher I was asked to attend a summer training session at the Houston Montessori Center, in order to work towards certification as a Montessori teacher. This training was required before I could become a full-time teacher at Parkview Montessori. I knew that this would mean a great sacrifice of time and energy, not only on my part but also on the part of my husband and children, who would remain in Tennessee while I sweltered through a summer of intense learning in Houston, Texas. What would impact me so much that I would be willing to make this sacrifice?

When I had completed my interim position I knew that I had experienced teaching in a manner that made sense for both my students and me. I wanted to understand why a Montessori classroom was different from traditional classrooms, and I wanted to continue to feel as if I was really making an impact in the lives of my students and in the world.

"Two rules come from the field of brain research and enrichment. One is to eliminate threat, and the other is to enrich like crazy." (Jensen, 1998, p.40) This quote from *Teaching With The Brain In Mind* by Eric Jensen, sums up for me the qualities which illuminate the philosophy and educational approach which Montessori created and inspired. A Montessori student is invited into an ordered, non-threatening classroom with fascinating materials which lead carefully, step by step, from concrete experiences to abstract thought. These learning materials invite students to see the universe as totally connected, and to see that they have a valuable place within.

When I completed the first week of training at the Houston Montessori Center, an overview of the preschool curriculum, I knew this would be an experience that would not only change my life but also give me the skills I needed to impact the lives of my students more effectively than did traditional teaching methods. I felt like I had learned more in one week than I had in twelve years of public school and four years of private college, and that was just the preschool curriculum. I looked forward to the rest of the training and wondered, "What is it about the Montessori method that helps to enhance a feeling of safety, while creating an environment full of educational opportunities?" Examining the idea of enhancing a feeling of emotional safety, I learned about the concepts of observation, the cycles of the classroom, teaching respect, a peaceful environment, and the use of Brain Gym, a program which uses movement to increase learning ability. I searched for ways that the classroom environment could be enriched through the unity of the curriculum, the introduction of conflict resolution skills, and the incorporation of traits that have come to define the Montessori method.

I developed more of an understanding of the Montessori Method after attending a special evening hosted by the Houston Montessori Center called a "Discovery Journey". This evening allowed me the opportunity to experience the entire scope of the curriculum from preschool through high school. There I saw that some of the same materials that were used in the preschool classroom were used throughout the curriculum, and even in the high school environment. This use of the same materials for different purposes seemed to create a feeling of safety and recognition, and also taught that something familiar that has in essence been "understood" before could still offer new lessons and insights. This is an incredible idea; especially in a time when as a society we seem obsessed with conquering and moving on to the next new thrill.

One of the lessons I found very interesting was the importance of observation. Maria Montessori addresses this idea in her book, *To Educate the Human Potential*.

> In the advanced primary stage, the first step to take in order to become a Montessori teacher is to shed omnipotence and to become a joyous observer. If the teacher can really enter into the joy of seeing things being born and growing under his own eyes, and can clothe himself in the garment of humility, many delights are reserved for him that are denied to those who assume infallibility and authority in front of a class.
> (Montessori, 1948/2002, pgs. 83, 84)

One of the ways in which I tried to increase my own powers of observation throughout the summer and outside of the formal classroom setting was by spending some time outdoors every day sketching the clouds. I would then record whatever thoughts came to me as a result of observing the clouds. This meditation helped me to realize that even though some things seemed to stay the same, they were actually moving and changing quite quickly and that only close observation could show how and why things happen.

This lesson has served me well in the classroom when watching students interact with Montessori materials and with one another. An example of this was a student who suddenly became very angry and began acting rudely toward another student. Stopping and looking at the situation I realized that he was acting out of frustration because my assistant had given him a book to read that was far beyond his ability level. His angry actions toward the younger student were actually a result of the anger and frustration he was feeling towards himself. Observing the situation closely had allowed me to ignore his rudeness and go directly to the root of the problem.

A book that we read during the summer training at the Houston Montessori Center was, *Theories of Development,* by William Crain. Reading this book helped me to learn more about the ideas of different theorists and to see how Montessori learned from those ideas and expounded on them. One of the major issues at the school where I am employed is an effort to explain the Montessori approach of teaching reading to our school district's reading specialist. Crain gives a quick summary of this approach in his chapter on Montessori (Crain, 1980, p. 66) explaining Montessori's ideas of introducing small steps as an indirect preparation during sensitive periods in order to master all the sub skills necessary. This approach leads to an explosion into writing which progresses into reading. Learning about these concepts of sensitive periods, the planes of development, three period lessons, and the work cycle has made me more aware of the importance of understanding exactly where a child is in order to guide educational needs. In her book, *Discovery of the Child*, Montessori expounds on this idea:

> Because a child is himself unaware of his mission and of his internal needs, and adults are far from being able to interpret them, many conditions prevail both at home and in school that impedes the expansion of his infant life. The freeing of a child consists of consists of removing as far as possible these obstacles through a close and thorough study of the secret needs of early childhood in order to assist it. Such an objective demands on the part of an adult greater care for, and closer attention to, the true needs of a child; and, practically, it leads to the

creation of a suitable environment where a child can pursue a series of interesting objectives and thus channel his random energies into orderly and well-executed actions. (Montessori, 1912/2002, p. 63, 64)

It is as if the traditional role of a teacher has been expanded to be more like that of a doctor prescribing the correct medication and dosage for a patient. This individualized approach is very different from forcing information upon students just because it is the appropriate time of the year according to the scope and sequence of traditional education. I have discovered that the humble teacher observes the student, allowing the needs and interests of the student to guide the lessons and materials that are introduced. Following the student in this manner encourages a sense of belonging and serenity. Materials that are aesthetically pleasing invite students into a joyful experience of learning. The combination of a teacher who is willing to listen and observe what a student needs and desires, along with the ability to present materials in an appealing way provides foundation stones for an environment in which peace naturally develops. In my personal life becoming more aware of developmental stages helps me to take the occasional ill temperaments of my 14-year-old son with more grace, recognizing that his propensity for arguing and analyzing is a normal stage that he is going through. I have discovered that the more willing I am to let go of my own ego and observe closely, the more effective I become as a teacher and a parent.

I was fascinated by the bulb chart which Montessori used to explain human development. (Grazzini, 1996, p.23) Figure 1 illustrates the bulb chart used by Montessori. The bulb chart defines the stages of development using a drawing that looks similar to a daffodil bulb lying on its side. This organic approach reveals that even though it is hidden, there always exists a great potential for growth. The mind is constantly absorbing information from the environment. This information is organized by the brain and even though it seems dormant it will frequently be able to present itself in a way that is relevant.

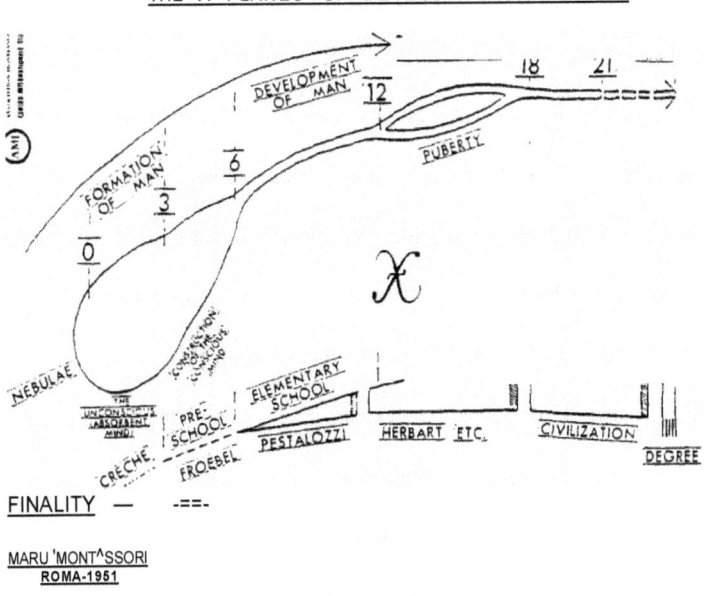

Figure 1. From Grazzini, C. (1996) *The Four Planes of Development*. The NAMTA Journal, Volume 21, No.2, p.223.

I see a clear connection between the bulb chart and Montessori's writings about *engrams*. According to Morris, the editor of *The American Heritage Dictionary* an engram is "A persistent protoplasmic alteration hypothesized to occur on stimulation of living neural tissue and to account for memory." (Morris, 1969/1975, p.434). Montessori states "The subconscious is full of these engrams, by which the intellect grows much more than by conscious memory." (Montessori, 1948/2002, p.13) She further explains:

> In accordance with these discoveries, we are now advised not to labor at memorizing some important piece of work, but rather to study it lightly and then set it aside for some days without forgetting it, so allowing the engrams time to organize themselves in concentration. (Montessori, 1948/2002, p. 15)

This explained why, in my experience, first graders often left for their winter break not being able to read yet returned two weeks later as readers. Perhaps it also explains why the Montessori test tube division material that was a struggle for me during the summer training course became very easy for me to explain in November even though I had not worked with the material since the summer course. These engrams are like shelves of knowledge in our brains, and the more information we place on any particular shelf the more we can organize and make sense of that information. Since I have a longtime fascination with dreams, their theories and meanings, and have kept dream journals for the past ten years, this study of engrams is something that I would personally like to continue studying, in order to find connections between engrams and dreaming. I am curious about whether dreaming is a vehicle for the subconscious to transport the rearrangements of engrams. This seems to me a good reason for the importance of rest for optimal learning experiences.

One of the teaching methods used in a Montessori school is an approach referred to as a three period lesson. A three period lesson is a natural opportunity to build up the shelves of knowledge in a non-threatening way. The first period involves presenting a piece of information using the statement, "This is…" During this period the teacher has knowledge of the information and is sharing it with the student. The second period is a time to assimilate the new information. The statement used during this period is," Show me…" This is practice time when the student is familiar with the material, but needs time to truly make it his own. The third period is an evaluation time and the question used is, "What is this?" It is an opportunity for the child to show mastery over new information. Depending on the information that is being learned, the time period for passing through each period will vary. The indirect preparation and sequential building of knowledge will also impact how quickly a student passes through each period. A student with a firm foundation will have a much easier time then a student who has not been exposed to the material during the developmentally appropriate sensitive learning period. A sensitive period is a time period when there is a strong internal desire to independently master a skill. John Chattin-McNichols describes the concept of sensitive period in the following quote:

> A sensitive period is a window in the development of the person. It is a genetic component, available to all humans regardless of cultural background. The use of the sensitive period is what will vary from culture to culture, family to family, even child to child within the same family. The sensitive period for language is a potential for language acquisition. The language or languages acquired will depend on the child's experiences with her environment. Many other sensitive periods are described by Montessori, the majority of them coming in the 3-6 period. (Chattin-McNichols, 1998, p. 37)

Montessori materials and lessons are designed to enhance the mastery of skills during sensitive periods. Some of the sensitive periods include a period for order, for details, for the use of the hands, for walking, for language, and for the acquisition of cultural experiences. I observe the effectiveness of prior learning during a sensitive period the most clearly with the students who have attended Montessori preschool. Students' exposure to Montessori materials during the sensitive periods allows the students to quickly grasp information and build on it, rather than struggling to learn the information once the sensitive period has passed. While we have a preschool at our school, it is state funded and designed, and unfortunately does not include a Montessori-based curriculum or philosophy. I can imagine that implementing a Montessori preschool program would be an immense benefit to our students who come to the upper levels from our own preschool.

TIES is an acronym for The Institute for Educational Studies, an internet based classroom associated with Endicott College comprised of students pursuing a degree in Montessori Integrative Learning. On the TIES online campus, Renee Williams, shared her experience of working with the preschool Montessori students at her school:

> I feel privileged to have the opportunity to impact the children at a young age. Although parents and outside forces have already had a great impact in shaping the child, developing intrinsically motivated children is surely a much easier task at three years old. Positive discipline (positive language and natural/logical consequences) is a major part of that process, especially when the child is being externally motivated by the teacher. In my classroom, we use encouragement rather than praise. I often

encounter children as young as three who are searching for praise ("Do you like my work?" or "Did I do a good job?") Their eyes are crying out for my approval. I refuse to put my opinion on them. I just reply with, "It looks like you did your best" or "You seem very proud of your work."

(ties-edu.org/campus/HMC2 Bohm, Peat-Briggs integrative seminar, 1:81)

A revolutionary idea for me was the importance of the work cycle for completion of learning. A work cycle is a period of independently choosing a task to focus on, working through and developing an understanding of that task to a point of internal satisfaction, which then often leads to a desire to share the new information with someone else. This cycle is another example of the importance of observation. A child up and walking around the room may be an indication of being in a false fatigue stage. Rather than trying to engage the student in work or activity, it is wiser to watch and let the student choose what work to do next. Stopping a student in the middle of the work cycle can lead to confusion and frustration. Recognition of this pattern has led me to see how many discipline problems can be avoided if a student is allowed to work through and complete an innate cycle of work. Montessori referred to this process as *normalization*: "And when they finished, they were rested and joyful; they seemed to possess an inner peace. It seemed that children were achieving, through intense work, their true or normal state; Montessori therefore called this process normalization." (Crain, 1980, p.72)

The work cycle is also an example of the overall tone that is set in a Montessori classroom. Teachers and other students alike respect and value one another. This respect is shown in many forms, like not disturbing someone who is working. This can come about by simply not interrupting them while they are working, or by using self-control when you are doing your own work. Self-control is exercised by practicing grace and courtesy to avoid stepping on the work of a classmate when walking through the classroom. One lesson that I give my students is to put several mats on the floor and have students think about and determine what would be the best traffic patterns in order to walk through the room and not disturb the work of others. This lesson provides an opportunity for students to walk through the class with intention, purpose, and consideration for others. These lessons help to develop inner composure and confidence. We also play several different quiet games in order to practice listening skills and using a quiet voice when talking.

In one of these games I stand outside the classroom and quietly call to students until they all have joined me. Another game, the whisper game, is started when students are in the circle and I turn to a student next to me and quietly give an instruction or make a comment. The student then turns and quietly tells the next student the same thing. The goal of this game is to learn to moderate the tone of voice so that only your neighbor hears you, and hears what you said accurately. This continues through the whole circle until the last person hears and repeats it to the class. This exercise requires patience, good listening skills, and using self control to modify your voice tone. Practicing grace and courtesy when walking through the classroom, and using a quiet voice help to form a community atmosphere of respect for one another and for learning.

The idea of the work cycle has been meaningful to me inside and outside of the classroom, as I realized that my own children also exhibited signs of being in work cycles. I noticed there were definite times they wanted to talk and interact with me and times they wanted to be left alone. Now when I want to talk to them I don't force my agenda on them. Instead I turn my attentions to other things knowing that soon they will come to me and want to talk. I found that observing these cycles provided our home with a more harmonious atmosphere.

A change in the way I greet students in the morning has been another way that I have implemented respect in our classroom. At the beginning of the school year I stood outside my door each morning to greet students and give them hugs as they entered the room. Over the months, though, I realized that if I pulled a small chair to the door and sat down, then I was truly meeting them eye to eye as they started the day. This simple change caused a great difference in my feelings of connection to the students and in their attitudes as they walked through the door into our classroom. It is my hope that by implementing even small changes like this into the classroom I am taking to heart the view of Philip Gang in his book, *Rethinking Education*, to provide first steps of respect.

> Self respect is an outgrowth of family and school experiences that dignify the opinions and attitudes of the individual. It emanates from a caring-loving environment wherein adults recognize the worth of the child. One does not educate for self respect, but enables self respect to develop. Students will have difficulty valuing the contributions of others unless they feel their own worth, so the family and school must provide the first steps towards developing respect for others, by valuing the worth of the individual. (Gang, 1989, p.49)

An important concept to remember is Gang's emphasis that self-respect is not a separate idea or lesson that can be taught. It needs to develop naturally through the attitudes of caring adults creating a loving environment.

Another example of incorporating respect in our classroom was the decision to change how students are called together for circle time. At first I would interrupt their work and verbally tell them to come to circle. This approach seemed to cause an immediate level of tension and disruption in our classroom. Taking a cue from Kathryn Miller, the teacher of our preschool overview during Montessori training at the Houston Montessori Center (HMC), I purchased a small music box. When I needed the students to come to the circle I turned on the music box. This had a calming effect on the children and they would get up and put away their work without talking and come to the circle.

Aline Wolf in her book, *Nurturing the Spirit*, gives an explanation of the importance of circle time:

> The circle itself is a wonderful symbol of community. It has no beginning or end, no front row or back row. Each sitting space is equal in rank, indicating that each person in the circle is equally important. The form of a circle has a long history of symbolizing togetherness. Many primitive cultures used it when drumming, chanting, and dancing, as well as for tribal meetings. Most Montessori classrooms have "circle" at least once a day. It is helpful, I think, to make the children aware of why this shape was chosen to gather everyone together. (Wolf, 1996, p. 124)

Community meetings are a part of this circle time. These community meetings provide a time to bond as a group. They also provide an opportunity for announcements, acknowledgements and a time to work through any issues that have come up in class that need to be addressed. Students taking the time to acknowledge one another and share their appreciation for one another is a simple yet powerful way to reinforce the worth and importance of each person. It reminds us on a daily basis that we work together to accomplish goals. The opportunity to problem solve together in community meetings is a great way to model conflict resolution in a peaceful manner.

The peaceful school environment and its potential for transforming society were attractions for me to the Montessori Method. Cosmic education, which could be described as the underpinnings of the entire Montessori curriculum, brings about a concept which Wolf describes:

> If everything in the universe came about from the same source-the original fireball that many believe preceded the creation of the stars-then we as human beings are related to all other human beings, as well as to the animals, plants, oceans and heavenly bodies. Therefore if we deliberately destroy nature or harm other living beings we might be ultimately destroying ourselves. This realization is an underlying principle for promoting peace, equality and care of the earth. (Wolf, 1996, p. 93)

Wolf's book was a great help to me in understanding ways to create a peaceful classroom. It is filled with exercises to use with students to help them resolve conflicts and see the importance of peace. Her book gives the format for using the "Peace Rose" to resolve conflict. (Wolf, 1996, p. 126) Our school uses a small teddy bear instead of a rose. Students begin the conversation holding the teddy bear and say, "When you…" "I felt…." "I would like for you to…" "Are you willing?" If the person who is listening would like to give an explanation for an action the teddy bear now passes hands and the same format is used to explain the other person's actions. This continues until everyone involved feels heard and a common solution is found. Using the Peace Bear has empowered my students to work out their own issues. It is a way of articulating the ideas that students care about both themselves and about the person with whom they are in conflict.

As a part of my master's work with TIES, I conducted an active interview with my school principal about peace education. An active interview is more of a conversation with another person in which the interviewer introduces a subject but then allows the person being interviewed to continue to expand on their experiences. The interviewer uses the information given to formulate new questions. The interview with my principal helped me to understand how important bringing peace into the awareness of students and their families can impact the world.

Active Interview

November 10, 2004

Interview between Ms. Crump and Peggy Smith

> *P.S.: M.C., what are some things that you have done personally to make a difference in the world?*
>
> *M.C.: Eight years ago I came to Parkview Montessori Magnet School after having taught um, for 17 years as a special educator. When I came here to the Montessori School I recognized the need to first research and*

understand Montessori. Then as a leader I knew that I had to embrace the philosophy. I did believe in it; I do believe in it. I embrace the philosophy of Montessori focusing on peace. I did a self-assessment on myself to make sure that I had peace within myself and that spiritually I was focused and had a connection for you know ...for the Peace Maker, and that is a personal conviction is to have my spiritual being, which is God in my life, so that would be a natural flow for me and I could practice that without having to work at it; I could just live it. So through my self-assessment, I was able to look at myself and to make sure that I had fully embraced peace within me, in my home, and to become a cheerleader, a drum major for peace. To live it, to practice it, to teach it, and to just to be about peace. Everywhere I go I try to just let the peace in me come through, even in conflict.

P.S.: Do you feel that before you did that self-assessment that there were already peaceful roots there and the self-assessment just helped to bring that more to awareness?

M.C.: I think the self-assessment allowed me to look at myself and to rethink and to soul-search, but also to understand it, how peace works, and to really know what is peace versus just a choice to do right and to do wrong. I think it's a conviction that lies within me that life is o.k.; it's a calmness that you get that is so spiritual and it is an individual grace that you get. It's not a group thing, so I think I was able to see myself and develop an appreciation that this was a good fit because I realized that I was in the right place, and it was easy to do, but then I was able to see it and maybe share it better and help others and explain it and pass it on. So that's kind of the way I look at it.

P.S.: How long did that self-assessment process take for you? Do you feel like it's still going on?

M.C.: I went through the self-assessment through my Montessori training. During it I took the peace education phase of training but it didn't come to reality and practice until I came to the job and I had to see it and I was challenged and I was able to teach it to others and to pass it on and help others get it because it's not something you can just learn. *(Pause)* You have to seek, and once you get it your whole world is different.

P.S.: What type of impact do you think Parkview Montessori is having on the world?

M.C.: I think we have revolutionized education through our approach of talking about peace, just talking about it, just saying the word. We promote it on our stationery, we promote it on communications that go out from the school, it's visible on the grounds, it's in the minds of children, we say it in the classroom, we talk about peace, we write peace, we practice peace, we teach conflict resolution. So I think that we are revolutionizing education because we believe that there should be peace, we think that children deserve a chance at a peaceful learning environment, and that if we teach our children, they will take it home, and they are helping us. So collectively we are making this world a peaceful place. I believe it was... um, Gandhi who said, "If there is going to be peace then it must begin with me." And peace is taking off in this building with the adults and we are passing it along to the children and we are educating our parents and our parents are going back to their jobs, and to their homes, and to their churches. So I think we are making an impact like a domino effect, touching the lives of people because we are living it and we are trying very hard to teach people to make a choice, and that there is such a thing as peace and you can have it.

P.S.: What things would you like to do in the future to increase peace in the world or to have Parkview make an impact on the world?

M.C.: I think hope is a big word here for me because a lot of people have given up and don't believe that things can happen. We are in a high poverty section of this city. I would like to see crime dissipate; I would like to see families stay together. I'd like to see children come to school excited about life and worried about school work as opposed to their homes, and their parents, and the confusion they are seeing at home. I would like to see us educate parents and to say you owe it to your children to give them a peaceful world in the homes. I would like to see us model how to solve conflict as staff members and as children. I'd like to see our school be more visible in the community promoting peace and to encourage people to come in and see that children can come to school and work in a peaceful environment not because of the adults but because of the choices that they are making to be peaceful. I'd like to encourage other educators at other schools that you don't have to be a Montessori school to have a peaceful environment and you don't have to physically force children, but if you have peace within yourself you can expect peace from others because you can give away so much of yourself for others to catch on . So I want us to continue to be a driving force as teachers to educate by doing.

P.S. Can you give me any examples of how you've already seen some of those things occur?

M.C. Parents usually are the ones that I hear it from the most. Because they come in and say, " You know my child said, Mom, you need the peace rose that we use, or you need the peace bear, or mom, we shouldn't talk that way, or my teacher said, or my principal said, we should respect one another or ... this is not the way we do it." And we are teaching our children that even if you want to interfere or get your parents attention at home, there is a respectful manner to do that so that we are not provoking others to behave in a disorderly way and to… to first show respect. So we are getting a testimony mostly from our parents and we see it in our children, where teachers are saying, "That I see fewer and fewer conflicts." I get few referrals to the office, very few, because teachers are expecting it, they are living it, they are involving parents, they are instilling it in the hearts of children and that's where we want it, you know we believe in preparing children for life, not just for the moment, but giving them something that will stay with them, that will help them make *decisions in the absence of the teacher, in the absence of parents, so we do get reports daily. I can see it in the face of children, I can see it in the smiles now replacing frowns. I see it in children finishing work. I see it in them coming in the door, I hear kind words, "I love you." "Have a nice day!" They get excited; they talk about it, so I think it is definitely working.*

Nobel Peace Prize Project

I chose to broaden this awareness of peace for my students by choosing to create for HMC classified nomenclature labels, a timeline, and research forms which identify and educate students about specific Nobel Peace Prize winners. Peace is not ever considered a separate subject that is taught in the Montessori classroom; it comes about as a result of students being in a well-prepared environment in which they understand that they are both vital and valued. My project therefore should not be looked upon as a way to peace, but a way to make concrete some abstract ideas about peace. This project allowed me to develop an understanding of what it was like for students to experience an educational material that taught them about Nobel Prize winners, and its effect on their perspectives about the world. I was especially interested in giving students a frame of reference for world events based on the lives of peacemakers

When I was in the sixth grade I was inspired by a thought by the Roman philosopher, Seneca. The thought included the idea that I should live my life in a way that it would be beneficial not only to me but also to others. This took hold in my young heart and started a lifelong desire to live my life in such a way that I would not just be taking up space on this planet but actually making a difference. That was the same year I decided that I wanted to be a teacher. One of the things that attracted me the most to Montessori education was the philosophy that the way to make the world a more peaceful place is through the education of the child. Recently I was able to attend a lecture given by Nobel Peace Prize winner Jody Williams, where she challenged, "If each one of us or even just handfuls found a way to make the world a better place, can you imagine the difference we would make." (Jody Williams, University of Tennessee at Martin, lecture, November 8, 2004)

My idea was that students could benefit from both the opportunity to develop in an environment that nurtures peace and by learning stories of real people who have spent their lives choosing ways to bring about peace, to inspire the students' imaginations of how to reach out to the world once they have left the Montessori environment.

Methods

In his book, *Researching the Lived Experience*, Max van Manen suggests an approach of using thematic analysis for uncovering meaning. This is the approach that I used to guide my research. "Themes are the stars that make up the universe of meaning we live through. By the light of these themes we can navigate and explore such universes." (Van Manen, 1997, p.90) Three interpretive processes have been used to uncover themes that surfaced through the gathered research information. These themes as suggested by Van Manen (1997, pgs. 92, 93) are the wholistic or sententious approach, the selective approach, and a detailed line-by-line approach.

In the introduction of *The Peace Book*, Louise Diamond states, "To live a culture of peace in the midst of war is an act of great simplicity, for you are proving that one person can make a difference." (Diamond, 2001) As children grow and develop, I believe they seek out role models to help guide their way. My project was an effort to introduce students to positive role models that can inspire them. Specifically, students were introduced to winners of the Nobel Peace Prize through the use of stories, nomenclature, timelines, research and dramatic interpretation.

Through this study I have gained an understanding of what it was like for students to experience peace education through materials created to teach them about Nobel Prize winners and how it changed their perspectives about the world. Through this study, each of the students has had an opportunity to realize that they can have a positive impact on the world. Studying this topic also provided an opportunity to see how it impacted the larger community. Student interviews indicated that there was a greater interest in solving problems peacefully. Families were able to see a difference as a result of their students experiencing these materials. As a teacher I felt that the Nobel Peace Prize Study created a more peaceful climate and peace-oriented focus for our classroom.

A variety of methods were used to accomplish this goal. A specific group of students were chosen to create active interviews that were guided by the following questions:

When you learned about Nobel Prize winners, what were some ways that you saw that they made a difference in the world? Which of the winners impressed you the most and why? What do you think made these people do something special for the world around them? How has studying about Nobel Peace Prize winners helped you to see that even just one person can make a difference in the world? What are some ways that you feel that you might could change the world to make it a more peaceful place?

Their research was collected to determine the things they felt were important about various prize winners. The research form that students used included this format:

Name of Nobel Prize Winner:

Birth date:

Year of death:

Year they won the Nobel Prize:

Why they won the Nobel Prize:

When students shared their research information, dialogue that followed was recorded to gain insights about what they learned and new perspectives they gained as a result of learning about these Nobel Prize winners.

After reading more about Nobel Peace Prize winners and completing their research forms, students did a dramatic interpretation of a specific Nobel Laureate for our school's Celebration of Learning, a presentation students make every nine weeks to share what they have been learning in their classrooms, with an audience of their peers, parents, and community members. Students also hosted a special night for their parents and community members in which they presented the information they learned about a specific Nobel Peace Prize winner in a creative manner of their choosing. Some students chose to do a dramatic interpretation; others created a game to share, or created art projects or oral reports.

Specific parents were chosen to do active interviews with using the following questions:

We have been studying Nobel Peace Prize Winners. What are some ways your child has brought this topic up at home? In what ways do you feel like studying this topic will be or has been beneficial to your child? Are there any ways that you have been impacted by your child's study of Nobel winners? Are there any ways that you personally try to make the world a more peaceful place?

Hermeneutic

Thematic analysis has been used to bring meaning to the information and interviews that were collected. Three interpretive processes have been used, as suggested by Van Manen in his book *Researching the Lived Experience* (2003, pgs. 92, 93), to uncover themes that ran consistently through my gathered information.

In using the wholistic approach, information has been distilled into a phrase that contains the essence of that experience. These phrases have been compared to uncover a common theme. The selective reading approach has been used to pinpoint specific ideas that seemed vital to the meaning of each experience. A detailed reading approach allowed the examination of each sentence in a research or interview to unlock crucial aspects of the experience that was described. The combination of these three approaches has allowed an opportunity to discover what it was like for the children to experience peace education through their interaction with materials created specifically to learn more about Nobel Peace Prize winners.

Student Interviews

My first active interview about the Nobel Peace Prize Project was with a female third-grade student.

> *Ms. Smith: "Sharon, when you learned about Nobel Peace Prize winners, what were some ways that you saw that they made a difference in the world?"*

Sharon: *"They made things better."*

Ms. Smith: *"Which of the winners impressed you the most and why?"*

Sharon: *"Jody Williams, because she helped ban land mines, and if people stepped on them they would blow up."*

Ms. Smith: *"What do you think made these people do something special for the world around them?"*

Sharon: *"So the world could be a better place."*

Ms. Smith: *"How has studying about Nobel Peace Prize winners helped you to see that even just one person can make a difference in the world?"*

Sharon: *"They made the world happier."*

Ms. Smith: *"What are some ways that you feel that you might could change the world to make it a more peaceful place?*

Sharon: *"Trying to work out things myself before getting help."*

Ms. Smith: *"How do you think that would make the world a more peaceful place?"*

Sharon: *"I don't move around as much so our room is quieter."*

Ms. Smith: *"Are there any ways that you try to encourage peace with your friends in our classroom?"*

Sharon: *"I tell them when something is inappropriate for them to do."*

Ms. Smith: *"Do you also try to be a good example?"*

Sharon laughs then says, *"No, not really."*

Ms. Smith laughs also, then says, *"Do you think you could be a good example of how to be peaceful?"*

Sharon: "Yeah, probably."

Ms. Smith: "Thanks for letting me interview you Sharon."

Sharon: "O.K."

My second active interview was with a second-grade boy, Chris.

Ms. Smith: "When you learned about Nobel Peace Prize winners, what were some ways that you saw that they made a difference in the world?"

Chris: "Umm. They did good."

Ms. Smith: "Which of the winners impressed you the most and why?"

Chris: "President Jimmy Carter, because that is who I did for my presentation."

Ms. Smith: "Why did you choose him for your presentation?"

Chris: "He was my mom's favorite president."

Ms. Smith: "He was mine too. I've met him before and he is a very nice man."

Chris: "Cool."

Ms. Smith: "Why do you think the Nobel Peace Prize winners chose to do something special for the world around them?"

Chris: "Because they thought the world was bad when they were a kid or something."

Ms. Smith: "What are some ways that you feel that you might could change the world to make it a more peaceful place?"

Chris: "Become president, but I probably wouldn't really do that."

Ms. Smith: "Is there something you might really do?"

Chris: "Maybe make comic books about peace."

Ms. Smith: "That sounds like a great idea. I look forward to reading them. Thanks for letting me interview you."

My third interview was with Maria, a third-grade student.

Ms. Smith: "Maria, when we studied Nobel Peace Prize winners, what were some ways that you saw that they made a difference in the world?

Maria: "How they made it more peaceful and helpful for people."

Ms. Smith: "Which of the winners impressed you the most, and why?"

Maria: "Mother Teresa, because she was a Christian, and she stayed with people that were about to die and helped them to believe in God."

Ms. Smith: "What do you think made the Nobel Peace Prize winners do something special for the world around them?"

Maria: "Because they knew how people felt and what they wanted, and they had a good heart and wanted to help them."

Ms. Smith: "How has studying about Nobel Peace Prize winners helped you to see that even just one person can make a difference in the world?"

Maria: "I don't know."

Ms. Smith: "Is there a way that you personally would like to be able to make the world a peaceful place?"

Maria: "I would like to build a good place for people that aren't wanted to go and make them feel like a family."

Ms. Smith: "Do you think that there are a lot of people out there that don't feel like they have a place to go, and that feel lonely inside?"

Maria: "Yeah, I think so."

Ms. Smith: "That makes me feel sad. What do you think causes people to feel that way?"

Maria: "I think that they probably did not have parents that were kind to them."

Ms. Smith: "Maria, I think it would be wonderful if you were able to build a place like that for people to go to. Thank you for letting me interview you."

My fourth interview was with a first-grade student, Leigh.

Ms. Smith: "Leigh, when you learned about Nobel Peace Prize winners, what were some ways that you saw that they made a difference in the world?"

Leigh: "Sometimes they helped children."

Ms. Smith: "What were some ways that they helped children?"

Leigh: "They gave them food and a place to live."

Ms. Smith: "Why do you think they did those things?"

Leigh: "So they could make the world more peaceful. There would be no more fights and wars. Fights waste time."

Ms. Smith: "That happens in our classroom sometime, doesn't it? We have to stop and wait for things to get peaceful."

Leigh: "Yeah."

Ms. Smith: "When we studied about Nobel Peace Prize winners did it help you to see that even one person can make a difference?"

> Leigh: "Yeah, because it was like you said that if we do something for peace it helps make a difference and when we all do it, it makes a big difference."
>
> Ms. Smith: "Wow, you really remembered that well. Leigh, if you could do something to make the world more peaceful what are some things that you would do?"
>
> Leigh: "I would give poor people a home, and food, and stuff they need."
>
> Ms. Smith: "You know Leigh, I want you to know that every day I see you being peaceful in our class, and reaching out and being friends to everyone in our class and I really appreciate that you are already a peacemaker."
>
> Leigh: "Thank you."

Student Research

The students were asked to choose a specific Nobel Peace Prize winner to do research on and then give a presentation to an audience made up of their families, their peers, and community members about their prize winner. The students were given very broad guidelines of how they could present the information about the winner that they chose to research. Some students chose to dress up in costume and do dramatic interpretations; some created a three-dimensional project to share; others came up with a game show format to encourage audience participation. The following poem was read by a third-grade student, John.

Cordell Hull

I'd like you to take a moment to mull with me

About a man named Cordell Hull

Who was from Tennessee.

He started out poor in a rented log cabin,

But he looked around and said,

"This ain't happening"

So he got an education,

And he helped our nation.

He wanted to teach,

But he had even farther to reach.

So he became a lawyer, then a politician.

He was a man with a mission.

He was a man with a plan

That ended up grand.

He was a great sensation.

He helped to start the United Nations.

So think ahead and maybe you will be… A Nobel Peace Prize winner

from Tennessee.

Presenting the information they had learned in a creative manner helped students to become personally attached to the Nobel winner that they chose to present. Students and audience members alike gained a new appreciation and respect not only for these peacemakers but also for each other.

Parent Interviews

Mrs. Jones has a first-grade student in my classroom. Her daughter chose to do a presentation on Archbishop Desmond Tutu.

Ms. Smith: "*During our classroom study of Nobel Peace Prize winners, were there any discussions that came up at home as a result of this study?*"

Mrs. Jones: "*Anna and I searched the Internet and read about several Nobel Peace Prize winners. She chose Desmond Tutu because he reminded her of Martin Luther King Jr.*"

Ms. Smith: "*In what ways do you feel this study has been beneficial to your child?*"

Mrs. Jones: "*It increased Anna's willingness to want to research information and it increased her reading. I think by participating in the oral presentation, Anna is more comfortable now with standing before an audience. I think she really liked the attention she got during the presentation.*"

Ms. Smith: "*She was adorable in her costume, and I think the music in the background added a nice touch.*"

Mrs. Jones: "*Uh-huh.*"

Mrs. Smith: "*Are there any ways that you personally try to make the world a more peaceful place?*"

> Mrs. Jones: "I teach my children and try to demonstrate to them that we should try to treat everyone with respect regardless of their gender, race, or background."

The next interview was with the mother of Mandy, a first-grade student.

> Mrs. Smith: "During our classroom study of Nobel Peace Prize winners, were there any discussions that came up at home as a result of this study?"
>
> Mrs. Locke: "Mandy recognized Martin Luther King, Jr. on TV and told us several bits of information about him and the Peace Movement. The training in peaceful negotiations and the discussions in the Montessori way and the Peace Prize winners is something she mentions often."
>
> Ms. Smith: "In what ways do you feel this study has been beneficial to your child?"
>
> Mrs. Locke: "She is aware of people that many adults know nothing about. She recognizes names and faces of people on the TV or in books. She also uses many peaceful techniques to deal with others."
>
> Ms. Smith: "Can you give an example?"
>
> Mrs. Locke: "It has changed the way she deals with her little sister at home."
>
> Ms. Smith: "Are there any ways that you have been impacted by your child's study of Nobel Peace Prize winners?"

Mrs. Locke: "In working on the presentation, she chose a person I did not know. We learned together. I was also amazed at her knowledge and questions. She understood a great deal of the information we found and asked some good questions about things that confused her."

Ms. Smith: "Are there any ways that you personally try to make the world a more peaceful place?"

Mrs. Locke: "I think that trying to be a Christian example as a person and mother is very important. We have the opportunity to display, teach, and live the example of the ultimate "peace" bearer. Jesus gave us the best example. I think for me in particular, I have a strength in dealing with children. I do not tolerate "unpeaceful" children. I want to encourage them to show self control and act in polite ways. I feel like I encourage those around me by showing that behaved children are formed by consistent and expected discipline."

Ms. Wade's daughter, a third-grade student researched Jane Addams.

Ms. Smith: "During our classroom study of Nobel Peace Prize winners, were there any discussions that came up at home as a result of this study?"

Ms. Wade: "Yes. We discussed other prize winners also and we also went to the library. My sisters and I had no idea who Jane Addams was, so we learned a lesson too!" (Laughter)

Ms. Smith: "In what ways do you feel this study has been beneficial to your child?"

Ms. Wade: "She was able to learn that there were a lot of people who made it possible for them to have schooling, and their struggles made a way for them to be able to have this as well as freedom."

Ms. Smith: "Are there any ways that you have been impacted by your child's study of Nobel winners?"

Ms. Wade: "Yes. It made me think more about peace and ways I can be peaceful."

Ms. Smith: "Are there ways that you personally try to make the world a more peaceful place?"

Ms. Wade: "Yes, I try to help a lot of friends and family, even leaving myself in a spot sometimes; I know God has got my back."

Ms. Smith: "Thanks Ms. Wade, I appreciate you working with Tanya on this project."

The following interview was with Mr. Wilton; his son is a second-grade student.

Ms. Smith: "During our classroom study of Nobel Peace Prize winners, were there any discussions that came up at home as a result of this study?"

Mr. Wilton: "I had a discussion about freedom and the civil rights movement. All black people didn't have equal rights like the white people did. Blacks was treated unfairly. Black people was killed, for no reason."

Ms. Smith: "In what ways do you feel this study has been beneficial to your child?"

Mr. Wilton: "My child has the freedom to sit on a bus, and drink water out of the same water fountain as white kids do, it was important for us to remember that and why that is."

Ms. Smith: "Mr. Wilton, are there any ways that you have been impacted by Travis's study of Nobel winners?"

Mr. Wilton: "I have been impacted by remembering that I have the freedom to speak, and the freedom to do what ever I want to do in this world."

Ms. Smith: "Are there ways that you personally try to make the world a more peaceful place?"

Mr. Wilton: "Umm, I just want people to get along with each other. I try to help them do that."

Ms. Smith: "What are some ways that you try to do that?"

Mr. Wilton: "Umm, just being easy to get along with and talking with them."

Ms. Smith: "Thank you for your time Mr. Wilton; I appreciate you being an involved parent."

Mr. Wilton: "That's what it's about. The kids and all."

Wholistic Interpretation

In approaching the study of Nobel Peace Prize winners in a wholistic way, it can be seen that even as our class was studying about how an individual person can make the world a better place, we were also seeing that we were simultaneously being impacted and having an impact on each other and on the lives of the people that we touched. It was as if we were all ingredients in a loaf of bread, each bringing our own talents and thoughts to the bowl, each of us being a leaven to make the other rise higher.

The project as a whole brought out pride and a sense of fun and adventure. As the teacher it was a delight to share materials with the students that had been created just for them. The students were excited to do research and to share the information they had learned. The parents learned along with us and were pleased with what their children had accomplished during their study. At a final meeting that was held at the end of the school year when asked, "What was the experience you enjoyed most during the school year?" A majority of the parents present talked about the Nobel Peace Prize project and presentations. They were impressed with how much all the students had learned individually and from each other. They talked about how much fun it was to get together and learn more about great peacemakers from the children.

Selective Interpretation

In looking through the different information gathered, there were some recurrent themes. Two of those themes seem to have been that to make the world a better place involves both being peaceful yourself, and then reaching out to others. In the interview with Sharon she indicated that to make the world a better place she could "try to work out things myself before getting help." She felt this would make our room quieter because she wouldn't be moving around so much. In Maria's research she indicated that the reason she liked Mother Teresa was because "she was peaceful and loving." Leigh had internalized the idea that "if we do something for peace it helps make a difference, and when we all do something it makes a big difference." In the interview with Mrs. Locke, her way to make the world a more peaceful place included trying to be a Christian example as a person and mother. Mrs. Jones referred to reaching out to others by saying, "I teach my children and try to demonstrate to them that we should try to treat everyone with respect regardless of their gender, race, or background."

Mrs. Locke revealed that her daughter's study of peacemakers changed the way her daughter dealt with her younger sibling. Ms. Wade replied "I try to help a lot of friends and family even leaving myself in a spot sometimes; I know God has got my back." This theme of being at peace inside and helping others continued with Mr. Wilton. He felt that the way he tried to make the world a more peaceful place was "by being easy to get along with and helping others to talk things out."

Another theme that surfaced was the way families benefited from the study by learning together or learning more about each other. In the interview with Chris, he stated that he chose Jimmy Carter for his presentation because President Carter was his mother's favorite president. James was able to learn more about his mother's job working for our city doing landscaping and planting trees when he studied about the Green Belt Movement. He was very excited to learn how the trees planted by the Green Belt movement helped to save lives when the villages were hit by a tsunami.

Mrs. Jones stated "Anna and I searched the Internet and read about several Nobel Peace Prize winners." She added, "It increased Anna's willingness to want to research information and it increased her reading." Since Anna came to the first grade this year as a non-reader, anything that helped her desire to read was appreciated by her parents.

Mrs. Locke reported, "In working on the presentation, she chose a person I did not know. We learned together. I was also amazed at her knowledge and questions. She understood a great deal of information we found and asked some good questions about things that confused her."

Ms. Wade laughed when she talked about going to the library with her sisters so they could also learn a lesson about Jane Addams. Mr. Wilton talked about his discussions about the importance of the civil rights movement and how it has impacted the lives of black people today. It was very important to him to remember this and pass it along to his children.

Line-by-Line Interpretation

Maria chose to write a report on Mother Teresa that can be looked at line-by-line to determine some underlying themes.

(1) Mother Teresa's birth and place of birth are significant to us now.

(2) Her ordinary life did not give an indication of the impact she would someday make.

(3) At the time of transformation between adolescence and adulthood she dedicated her life to helping others.

(4) In her 40s she was well know for reaching out to some of society's most helpless victims.

(5) The world became aware of unconditional love because of her example.

(6) She experienced greatness because of her lifestyle.

(7) Her life was transformed into purity similar to that of Jesus.

(8) Even the dying were able to experience her kindness.

(9) The work she had accomplished had a transformative effect on the world and she was honored by being given the Nobel Peace Prize.

(10) The world experienced an awareness of the importance of her life.

(11) Her work was helpful in transforming the lives of others.

(12) Her death was a great loss to the world.

(13) Her death was seen as the ultimate transformation, as a freeing of her spirit to a better place.

Conclusion of Research Project

Creating and watching all the different aspects of my Nobel Peace Prize project had a transformative impact on my life. The night of the final presentations was an amazing experience for me. I was amazed at the work and excitement of my students, thrilled that so many people came out to support them, and overcome with the realization that here in very small bodies were very strong souls. As they shared their stories of these caring giants of the peaceful past I was able to glimpse at caring giants of the peaceful future.

Inspired by the positive outcome of the Nobel Peace Prize work, I decided that when the next year came around, instead of assigning homework on a nightly basis I would assign projects for students to work on each month at home and then they would bring in their work to share with the class at the end of the month. One of the aspects I love about the project idea is that everyone in the class learns from each other and we all learn more than if I tried to do all the research and present the information that only I could find. Projects are based on a major theme of the month, for instance planets and space, types of leaves, study of a country, interview with a governmental official or research of a governmental position, science experiments, Nobel Peace Prize winners, or maybe an art project from a specific time period.

I have been amazed at their excitement and creative expression. One first grader brought in a styrofoam representation of Saturn that he had hollowed out the inside and put in green and blue beads to represent how many Earths would fit inside of Saturn. It was beautiful and he was very excited and told us all about it. The other students take notes while each project is being explained. Their notes are artistic and insightful.

In my opinion, the most wonderful thing about the projects is that I learn so much and the students are proud to share their information with everyone. In a posting on the TIES website Mandy Denomme shared her experience with a school wide project.

> I am thinking about our school wide celebration we had this week. Our theme was "peace, grace and courtesy in the world". A perfect lead in to this seminar. I was honored by the creative level the students reached. The lesson for me was to allow them space and time to "pause" for them to be able to create together a dialogue of activity. They made plates (out of clay) of people who represented peace to them and then set a dinner table with the plates. It was beautiful. They filmed a video on the freedom riders, created sand Mandalas, wrote poems and letters to peacemakers in history, and more. Observing their creative dialogue about what to present and how, was fascinating. It followed Bohm's perceptions of collective participation and "bringing your assumptions together" and reaching common ground as a community. It was difficult to not become a leader but let them discuss it and "create something new". I enjoyed finding the

parallels in the readings and the theme of awareness kept occurring to me. The word awareness has several synonyms: aware, cognizant, conscious, sensible, awake, alert, watchful, vigilant. It is interesting that the word awareness can be represented as being knowledge, feeling or sense and action or all of the synonyms together. (ties-edu.org/campus/HMC2, Bohm, Peat-Briggs integrative seminar, 1:1)

An interesting thing happened after I started my own classroom projects: my curriculum coordinator was so impressed that she proposed that the whole school start doing collective projects on a regular basis. As I walk down the halls during a project week I am very touched by all the projects of the students in the whole school knowing that this started in my little classroom. Now we have projects created from a whole school from which we can learn. If I see a project that is especially interesting I ask that student if they will be a guest speaker in my classroom and my own students have become used to being guest speakers for other classrooms.

Brain Gym

One aspect of creating a peaceful environment that I encountered during my training at HMC was the use of P.A.C.E.: positive, active, clear, energetic. It is a four-step introduction to Brain Gym, a program that is expounded in the book *Brain Gym* by Dr. Paul Dennison and Gail Dennison. This program outlines the basics of *educational kinesiology*, the study of how movement affects education. An aspect of P.A.C.E. which I have found most helpful in my classroom is the *positive exercise* called *hook-ups*. Hook ups is an exercise involving crossing your arms, clasping your hands together, and pulling your hands close to your chest. I have found this exercise to be good for activating an emotional grounding which seems to center and calm both students and teacher alike. I have noticed that when I just need to clear my mind before opening my mouth, I will look down and realize my hands seem to have assumed a hook-up position of their own accord. To me, this reflects the concept of *body intelligence* which theorizes that the body will on its own seek to fulfill its needs. I found that P.A.C.E. was a method that incorporated physical movement to promote mental readiness for learning. It was easy for me to understand how the use of the Brain Gym program is a natural fit for a Montessori classroom, as it provides a way for individuals to seek and meet their own emotional and mental needs. I am very interested in learning more about the potential use of Brain Gym for students that struggle with learning disabilities. *Brain Gym for Educators* offers the following suggestions for helping these students:

> Children who do not complete the developmental transition from homolateral to contralateral movement in infancy commonly experience academic or movement difficulties later. Inability to cross the midline is typical of students who are labeled "learning disabled" or "clumsy." Brain Gym Midline Movements provide a way to complete any missed developmental stages and "catch up" in laterality skills at a later time. Each Brain Gym activity is designed to encourage completion of the missing movement patterns in the laterality development sequence, and to augment the student's ability to move or act across the processing midline for any area of endeavor. (Brain Gym for Educators, 2000 p.30)

These exercises bring about a physical progression to prepare the way for mental learning in much the same way as moving across the classroom with the Montessori math materials, the golden beads, gives a child a physical appreciation of the weight of a ten bar in comparison to the weight of the thousand cube. The golden bead is a small gold bead. A ten bar is a group of ten of these beads put together, and a thousand cube is a thousand of these beads put together in the shape of a cube. The thousand cube not only looks very different from a single bead but it also has more weight.

Unity throughout the Curriculum

Much of the joy and effectiveness of Montessori materials can be attributed to the integration of physical movement using tactile, hands-on materials to guide students in a sequential manner towards abstract thought. This integrative aspect of the Montessori classroom applies not only to the physical aspect of the materials but also to each of the learning strands working together. Students perceive learning that is not chopped up into arbitrary blocks of time but rather that all learning flows together, creating a connective web. Margaret Wheatley in her book *Leadership and the New Science* refers to this need for a connective process of learning:

> We can't use neat and incremental methods to make sense of the world any longer. We need to be experimenting with thinking processes that better suit our neural netlike brains, those processes that are open, nonlinear, messy, relational. As we develop these, we will learn new ways to process the mass of information that too often overwhelms us now. As we learn to deal with information on its own terms, we will come to treasure it as the essential partner that it is. (Wheatley, 1999, p. 109)

This beautiful connection is one of the reasons that teachers at my school had such a difficult time explaining our approach to reading to our school district reading specialist. She was afraid that we were not spending the 90 minutes daily which our district requires for teaching reading. When you look at the Montessori curriculum, though, you can see that reading is incorporated into every subject taught, whether that is matching geometry nomenclature, or reading information for filling out research forms. We felt that the case could be made that we were teaching reading all day long, far exceeding the required 90 minutes. According to Michael Duffy and D'Neal Duffy, this type of integration is one of the vital principles of the Montessori method:

> Whenever ties can be made between elements of the curriculum that reinforce each other, the learning is made more effective and interesting. Teachers should always strive to integrate the curriculum elements as much as possible, weaving them into a single fabric. (Duffy & Duffy, 2002, p.146)

This tapestry of learning creates students that can pull together connections to enrich the quality and enjoyment of their lives. In my opinion, one of the marks of an intelligent person is a well-developed sense of humor. The reason I find this to be true is because humor involves linking different aspects of life together. This is also an aspect of problem-solving, the ability to link and think outside the box. It seems to me that the Montessori curriculum lends itself easily to this process. A Montessori classroom is like a microcosm of the world. A student is able to walk around the room and see the connectedness of all things. This provides a sense of wholeness and an awareness of being a vital part of that whole. An example of this is the lesson for teaching the grammar symbol for the noun, which is a black triangle. The preface for this lesson is comparing a pyramid, which is very old and solid, to the noun, which is for naming; this was the first type of word that humans used. This connects nouns, geometric shapes, and ancient civilizations all in one lesson.

Another example of connection through the curriculum is the emphasis of etymology. Word roots and meanings are given to enhance the meaning of the subject being learned and to establish its relevancy with other subjects being taught. Timelines are used to give students a way to make connections of crucial events through history while using math to convey the amount of time that has passed by.

"Math also can be useful in the production of historical timelines that demonstrate the relative proportions of different eras." (Duffy & Duffy, 2002, p.30) Along with using timelines to show movement through time, a large emphasis is placed on clocks and calendars to tell time. The book *Robinson Crusoe*, by Daniel Defoe, is used to introduce the idea of recording the passage of time through journaling.

> There are presentations in the Montessori curriculum to familiarize the children with these concepts and introduce them into the way we measure and record time on our planet. The children learn about the months of the year, the days of the week, the seasons of the year, the counting of years and calendars. These concepts are presented in a series of lessons that examine the origin of the words, explore the history of the way we count the years and help the children master these critical pieces of information for keeping track of daily living. They are given a taste of what the very concept of "time" means, something that until then they have not consciously studied. (Duffy & Duffy, 2002, p.66)

Students in the classroom also participate in a *celebration of life* which involves making a timeline with pictures of their own life and a ceremony in which a flat wooden sun with a candle in it is placed in the middle of the circle of students. The months of the year are laid out around the sun. The child whose life is being celebrated then walks around the circle starting and ending on the month of birth. As the student being celebrated walks around the sun, the students in the surrounding circle sing a song about the earth going around the sun. When the child returns to the month of birth, a parent or the child, will talk about what happened during that specific year of the child's life.

I have come to understand that this process of recognizing the milestones in a student's life is not only a way to emphasis that the Earth rotates around the sun, or how we measure time through a year, but is most importantly a way of affirming that each person is valuable and has a place and a purpose in the world. Montessori's term for this idea is *cosmic task*:

> This is the cosmic task of humanity, to be the conscious witness and promoter of unity for the human race, all of life's forms and the universe itself. Montessori students are taught to see themselves as citizens of the world, a species within the family of living species on Earth and, ultimately, as descendants of the universe. (Duffy & Duffy, 2002, p. 128)

The cosmic task that Montessori seemed to understand to be her own was that of creating a more peaceful world through education. It was to this task that she dedicated her life. While her methods of teaching were brilliant, it was her commitment not only to her students, but to her passion for harmony throughout the world that truly challenges us even now.

> Never one to think in small terms, she saw her child-centered education as the way to radically transform society, so that humankind would be protected from the threat of self-destruction through warfare. For this

unique approach to peace, she was nominated three times for the Nobel Peace Prize. (Duffy & Duffy, 2002, pgs. 128,129)

My experience in learning about peace during my Montessori training led me to the conclusion that peace is the idea that you care more about the relationship with another person than simply having your own way. It is an understanding that peace is not the absence of conflict but rather the process of working through it. During the summer I had the opportunity to watch and participate in a peace dialogue that occurred between the HMC students that were in training for teaching high school students and the students training to teach at the elementary level. Some of the elementary trainees felt they were being treated rudely by the high school trainees, while some of the high school trainees felt like their territory was being invaded not realizing that their classroom was the only one with items needed by the elementary trainees. I also watched how several other tense issues were worked through in peaceful ways, and some that were not totally worked through but were dealt with in a peaceful way. Observing and learning from these experiences was one of the most valuable aspects of the training for me in Houston. I needed to comprehend and have experiences with conflict resolution on a deep emotional level in order to truly understand what I would be trying to teach my students. What I learned from these experiences is that people genuinely want to be heard and they want their feelings validated. They want to be understood. Sometimes this is enough and sometimes it is only the beginning, like a small candle lighting the vast darkness in a cave of despair. I discovered that sometimes the things that people seem the angriest and frustrated about are really a cover for deeper issues that either have nothing to do with the topic at hand, or that they are not emotionally ready to deal with. It is my hope that teaching peaceful communication skills will offer a way for students to effectively share their care and concern for one another in a way that will allow that small candle to shine with more brilliance. I may not be able to erase the effects of brokenness, but perhaps by being willing to actively listen and understand the things my students are saying and the things they are not saying, I can give them the strength to travel a little farther than they could have alone.

For me this is what Montessori meant when she referred to the idea of following the child. Instead of trying to make another person fit your mold, take the time to listen, to observe, to understand, before attempting your next move. This holds true whether teaching math operations, or coming to terms with a peaceful agreement that will satisfy everyone.

Common Characteristics of a Montessori Classroom Which Foster Peace

The way Montessori chose to study history through the needs of people is an opportunity to foster the idea of the unity of all people. It emphasizes the realization that throughout time, all over the world, people have had common needs. This also presents the idea that our culture has been built on the gifts and experiences of previous cultures. This method takes the idea that humans have fundamental needs, to a specific study of some of those needs and how humans have met them. A study is then made of how the need that was specifically met during that time and place might later impact the rest of humanity. This whole, part, back to whole, method is used extensively throughout the curriculum. Montessori found the study of culture is optimal in a child's life during the ages of six to twelve:

> Education between the ages of six and twelve is not a direct continuation of that which has gone before, though it is built upon that basis. Psychologically there is a decided change in personality, and we recognize that nature has made this a period for the acquisition of culture, just as the former was for the absorption of environment. (Montessori, 1948/2002, p.3)

An awareness of the internal needs of a child at each stage of development, and providing an environment that meets that need and expands a child's understanding of the world, are two ways in which education can provide a climate of peace for the child to grow in. In the book *Education and Peace*, Montessori identifies the importance of objects in the environment.

> The child cannot develop if he does not have objects around him permitting him to act. Until the present, it was believed that the most effective learning took place when knowledge was passed on directly to the child by his teachers. But it is really the environment that is the best teacher. The child needs objects to act; they are like nourishment for his spirit. (Montessori, 1949/1999, p.56)

Other characteristics of the Montessori environment involve the student moving independently through concrete to abstract lessons. When a lesson is first introduced manipulative objects are used to help explain a concept. An example of this are the fraction pieces, which are metal circles cut into various fraction sections. This material makes it very simple for students to recognize fraction equivalents. When manipulating this material they can see that two of the one half sections make up the same space as a whole circle. Using materials like these allows students the freedom to discover information on their own without a teacher helping them every moment. Eventually the student masters the skill being taught to a point where using the manipulative is tiresome and they prefer to work on the concept without use of the material.

Classrooms are often composed of more than one grade level. I teach in a classroom comprising students that range from six to nine years old, or what traditional schools would think of as first, second, and third grade students. This provides an individualized environment for students that may be intellectually, physically, mentally or emotionally above or below their actual age groups. The work they choose for themselves is based on their own desires and needs, not the needs of a preconceived, outside enforced standard.

The concept of the prepared environment is an aspect of Montessori education that I have come to appreciate. The prepared environment refers to an environment ready with everything needed to meet the child for the day. This involves a wide range of ideas, from making sure the pencils are sharpened and all needed supplies are available for the student, to the classroom being a physically and spiritually comfortable zone to enter. I have found in my own classroom that this requires coming to school early to ready myself mentally for the day and staying late after school to physically ready the room for the next day. Gathering all the necessary supplies, pencils, paper, and materials for new lessons are some of the ways I physically prepare the room. While this has been challenging, it certainly makes a difference on the days when I am able to do this. It helps me to remember that while the environment is crucial to setting the tone for the child, the adult provides a critical function through preparation, attitude, and example. Montessori had this to say about the role of the adult in the environment:

> I would not lead you to believe that this kind of environment works miracles all by itself and that the adult has no part to play in it. The adult does have a role to play. He must show the child how to use objects correctly; he must show him, for example, how to polish metal. And in order to do this, he must get all the necessary things ready-bits of rag, metal polish, and so on-and he should be quite 'finicky', so to speak, about the whole procedure, because it is this very meticulousness that arouses the child's interest. The child watches the adult working methodically and carefully repeats his actions methodically and carefully. (Montessori, 1949/1999, p.79)

Main Areas of a Montessori Classroom

Main areas of a Montessori classroom may include math, language, cultural, geography, history, and science. These areas have physical separations in the classroom, but in reality they all flow together, which is a unique and impressive aspect of the Montessori approach.

In the math area, addition fact exercises give students the opportunity to experience working with concrete materials that show addition horizontally, vertically, and with missing addends. This is to enable the students to transfer this knowledge slowly over from concrete experiences to abstract knowledge. There are two levels of addition, including static, which involves answers under nine, and dynamic, referring to answers higher than nine, requiring an exchange of numbers. Exchanging is the key to the hierarchy system of moving through higher numbers. Subtraction is also taught using concrete materials that lead to abstract knowledge. Word problems are an excellent way to include reading in the math curriculum. Word problems help the student visualize the answer. They also give students additional practice with their math facts.

During HMC training an emphasis was placed on the separation of math fact work and math operations work. These are separated because math operations introduce the concepts of math while fact work concerns the memorization of facts. After a concept is introduced and students understand, for instance what it means to add, then they can begin to work on fact work activities which help them memorize their addition facts.

Fraction work is introduced before fact work. This is because it is very concrete and easy to understand from day-to-day experiences. Relating to the idea of half of a sandwich or a fourth of pizza is something students are able to easily do. Using the geometric fraction circles is a time-consuming activity and especially helpful for first-year students who need a productive activity at the beginning of the year while they are becoming familiar with the classroom.

Geometry is a prime example of the integration of the classroom. Students match three dimensional shapes with cards that have the name of the shape, the etymology of the name, and the definition of the shape. For instance the hexagon shape would have an etymology label that identifies hex as coming from the Latin word six and gon from the Greek word for corner. A shape with six corners would be written on the definition card. Word etymology and definitions strengthen reading while the study of geometry creates an awareness of shapes all around them.

Etymology is also used extensively in the language arts section of the classroom. Function of words lessons introduce the vocabulary for the grammar which a student already innately understands. Given in small group lessons, the grammar boxes give purposeful movement for the reinforcement of the function of words lessons. It also provides intense sight word recognition practice. In Carole Chase's book *Madeline L' Engle {Herself}*, insight is given as to the importance of vocabulary.

> The more our vocabulary is controlled, the less we will be able to think for ourselves. We do think in words, and the fewer words we know, the more restricted our thoughts. As our vocabulary expands, so does our power to think. (Chase, 2001, p.283)

History of language lessons are important to show students that our language has a history that comes from other people and supports the idea of one culture building on another. Elisabet Sahtouris, in the book *EarthDance*, promotes the crucial idea that we need to honor, support, and learn from other cultures.

> Diversity is crucial to nature, yet we humans seem desperately eager to eliminate it, in nature and in one another. This is one of the greatest mistakes we are making. We reduce complex ecosystems to one-crop monocultures, and we do everything in our power to persuade or force others to adopt our languages, our customs, our social structures, instead of respecting their diversity and recognizing its validity. (Sahtouris, 2000, p.12)

Research activities offer students an opportunity to continue to build respect for the diverse world around them while increasing their written communication skills to tell about what they are learning. It increases vocabulary and gives practice with editing skills. In my classroom it also offers students an opportunity to practice their computer skills. Students start by writing simple one-word answers. This leads to simple sentences, then progresses to complete paragraphs. They enjoy typing up their research, which they print out and illustrate.

The topics for research often come from the cultural areas of the classroom, including geography, zoology, and botany. In the fall every year our school hosts a multi-cultural market for the community. Community members are invited in to tour booths that are filled with student research and projects based on a country of the world that the students of each class have chosen to learn about. This experience not only gives them practice with research; it also widens their perspective and comprehension of the diverse cultures of the world. I believe that research teaches students how to learn new subjects on their own. It is a big world, but if my students have frequent opportunities to experience the ways and means to get the information that they need, then there is a sense of peace that understanding and knowledge is always possible.

It is not possible that I could teach my students everything that they need to know in their lives however, if I can give them a strong base to stand on, the tools they need to help them search, and the confidence that they are capable, then I believe I will not only be accomplishing my own cosmic task, my understanding of why I exist and how I contribute to life, but my students will be able to recognize theirs also.

Students entering a Montessori environment are given the opportunity to experience knowledge of the world around them gently, like the unfolding of a beautiful rosebud. Each step they take leads to new understanding and provides a path for future learning. Gently, without feeling threatened or overwhelmed by too much information at one time, students learn about the world and develop a healthy sense of self at the same time. I believe that whether students are learning about addition or how to get along with one another, the Montessori curriculum and philosophy offers a discovery journey that will last them, and me, a lifetime.

Exploring The Transformation Of A New Montessori Teacher

Entering my second year of Montessori teaching I noticed a subtle but crucial change in my answer to the common question, "What do you do?" The previous year, the answer to that question was, "I teach at a Montessori school." Now the answer to that question has changed to, "I am a Montessori teacher." This change in my answer has left me with the desire to look back and explore the experiences which transpired, leading me from teaching at a Montessori school to being a Montessori teacher.

At the beginning of the Montessori school year, classification games are a significant part of the curriculum. These games allow students an opportunity to discover ways to classify the world around them. Classifications of living beings, the five kingdoms, and other categories may guide a student into new ways of observing and understanding life. As I look back at my first year of teaching in a Montessori school, my training, and my graduate studies, I realize there have been definite paradigm shifts which have led me from the category of being a teacher in a Montessori school to becoming a Montessori teacher. To investigate this idea I will be looking closely at the things I read, the people I encountered, other things I encountered that coincided with these experiences, ways I felt that my perspectives have changed, and the impact I seemed to have on others. My desire is that, after looking closely at these topics, I will be able to more clearly understand and describe to other people what it means to me to be a Montessori teacher.

Readings

Looking back over the past year, I realize that many different books have taken up residency beside my bed to be absorbed and contemplated. These books have ranged from *On Dialogue* by David Bohm, *The Discovery of the Child* by Maria Montessori, *Nurturing the Spirit* by Aline Wolf, to *Researching Lived Experiences* by Max van Manen, along with many other thought-provoking readings.

One thought from the book *On Dialogue* which had a dramatic impact on me was from the foreword on page x regarding the thoughts of Patrick de Mare, M.D.

> The notion of "impersonal fellowship" suggests that authentic trust and openness can emerge in a group context, without its members having shared extensive personal history. In addition, the "theory of the microculture" proposes that a sampling of an entire culture can exist in a group of twenty or more people, thereby charging it with multiple views and multiple theories. (Bohm, 2003, p.x)

The reason for this passage's impact was due to experiences I have personally had while participating in dynamic group activities and how close this brought me to complete strangers in a short time. This theory of an entire culture existing in a group of twenty or more people helped me to realize that if true harmony can be developed in a classroom, the possibility of it occurring on a larger scale in the world could also be true. In dynamic group activities, the keys to drawing closer seem to be having a common goal, and taking the time to get to know the other people in the group rather than prejudging them.

I was very interested in how the group dynamics in my classroom changed with the addition of a new student in January. This student was believed to have been emotionally disturbed. Watching how the students related to her amazed me. I kept thinking these students were learning how to be kind to someone that is not kind to them, and how to redirect her to make better choices, and now they would have these personal communication skills to use for the rest of their lives.

An interesting phenomenon I noticed was that one child with previous negative behavior traits had to mature and behave in more appropriate ways because no one had the energy to cope with two people exhibiting malformed temperaments. This made me wonder: in any group of twenty people is there almost automatically some type of negative behavioral characteristic? Is it necessary in some way to balance the group and provide a sort of chaos? John Briggs and F. David Peat reveal the science of chaos in this statement:

> Chaos science focuses on hidden patterns, nuance, the "sensitivity" of things, and the "rules" for how the unpredictable leads to the new. It is an attempt to understand the movements that create thunderstorms, raging rivers, hurricanes, jagged peaks, gnarled coastlines, and complex patterns of all sorts, from river deltas to the nerves and blood vessels in our bodies.
> (Briggs & Peat, 2000, p. 2)

On an online posting, Allison Matulli brought up more ideas about chaos theory:

> Originally, chaos theory was employed to comprehend the movements that create thunderstorms, raging rivers, and hurricanes. More recently, chaos theory is applied to everything from medicine to warfare to social

dynamics and theories about how organizations form and change. However, today there is a grave change in the wind; chaos is undergoing an evolution from a scientific theory into a cultural metaphor. And with this shift, the Western world's oversimplification of what "it" is begins to wilt. Chaos is no simple one-dimensional explanation.

(Bohm, Peat-Briggs integrative seminar, 1:58)

This idea gave me a very different perspective on behavior and group dynamics. Now it seems to me that chaos theory could suggest that adjusting to aberrant behavior helps develop sensitivity and creative responses for problem solving. It gave me permission to be at peace in stressful situations. Instead of looking at them as problems it became easier to see them as opportunities for growth, perhaps even as necessary ingredients to create a stronger whole.

The concept of changing perspective when dealing with a problem was also looked at in another section of the book *On Dialogue:*

> Rather, you may suspend the activity, allowing it to reveal itself, to flower, to unfold, and so you see the aggression and it's actual structure inside of you. Movements are taking place inside of you- physical feelings-the heartbeat, the blood pressure, the way you breathe, the way your body feels tense; and also the kinds of thoughts that go along with these feelings. You can observe these things, be aware of them, and of their connection. (Bohm, 2003, p.73,74)

I first became aware of this idea years ago from reading the reality therapy concepts espoused by David Reynolds in his book *Constructive Living*. (Reynolds,

1997/2002). Reynolds ideas for understanding emotions were an epiphany in my life that I still try to hold on to. Instead of being angry or hurt, I can breathe in and observe what my body is experiencing and think, "Oh, this is anger, which is interesting." In the process I have become less afraid of my own emotions by learning how to deal with life situations with less anxiety. In the classroom, thinking about this concept encouraged me to be more observant of my students rather than automatically reacting to their behavior. By slowing down and observing, I noticed new avenues for me to honor and respect my students in ways that had never occurred to me before. The most powerful of these avenues was the opportunity to recover peace within myself and pass that peaceful energy along to my students. Julia Thiele remarks about dialogue in the following online comment:

> The idea of dialogue as a process in making something new and collaborative, I found very exciting. I think both at home and in educational settings this will make for something that genuinely makes a difference. Yet how frail we seem as human beings when we consider our difficulty in stepping away from our assumptions, without defensiveness and being truly open to other ideas.
>
> (ties-edu.org/campus/HMC2, Bohm, Peat-Briggs integrative seminar, 1:3)

This synergetic connection of being unique and yet a vital part of the whole is expounded on in the book *The Seven Lessons of Chaos*:

> Our creative moments-whether it is looking freshly at a tree or coming to a new understanding about our lives-are moments when we are in touch with our own authentic truth, when we experience our unique presence in

> the world. But, paradoxically, the experience of a unique presence is also often coupled with a sensation of ourselves as indivisible from the whole. (Briggs & Peat, 2000, p.28)

I believe a tremendous part of my transformation over the past year has been a stirring of my soul to seek peace and share the importance of peace with others as if all our lives depend on it. *The Seven Lessons of Chaos* deals with the concept of using "*butterfly power*" a term coined from an old Chinese proverb.

> Measured against the great forces at play in the world, a butterfly fluttering its wings doesn't seem to possess much power. But an ancient Chinese proverb says that the power of a butterfly's wings can be felt on the other side of the world.
>
> Chaos has shown ways in which this proverb may be literally true. As a metaphor, the chaos idea changes the way we think about power and influence in the world and in our individual lives. (Briggs & Peat, 2000, p.31)

It is my hope that my slowing down, honoring my students, and seeking peace within myself will indeed create an energy wave of peace that will be transformative not only for me, but also for many other lives. For me, the idea of butterfly power means that even the small steps that I take to increase peace in the world may ultimately be the cause of numerous positive changes that I may never even be aware of. I explored this idea in more detail after watching the DVD produced by Philip Gang and Marsha Morgan *Introduction to Montessori Radical Education* (Gang & Morgan, 2003). My initial response to this presentation could be summed up in one word: "*honor*." It opened up for me questions of, "How do we teach children how to honor the Earth, themselves, and each other, and how do we as adults do the same thing?" It made me think of a section of the *Desiderata* by Max Ehrmann:

> Beyond a wholesome discipline, be gentle with yourself. You are
> a child of the universe no less than the trees and the stars; you have
> a right to be here. And whether or not it is clear to you, no doubt the
> universe is unfolding as it should. Therefore be at peace with God,
> whatever you conceive Him to be. And whatever your labors and
> aspirations, in the noisy confusion of life, keep peace in your soul.
> (Ehrmann, 1979, p.11)

It has occurred to me that closely linked with finding inner peace is this idea of being aware of the universe around me and my impact on it. Seeking ways to work in connection with the natural world has been a topic of much thought and conversation during my process of trying to understand deeper implications of peace. Thomas Berry states these thoughts so well in his book, *The Great Work*:

> We cannot doubt that we too have been given the intellectual vision,
> the spiritual insight, and even the physical resources we need for carrying
> out the transition that is demanded of these times, transition for the period
> when humans were a disruptive force on the planet Earth to the period
> when humans become present to the planet in a manner that is mutually
> enhancing. (Berry, 1999, p.11)

Berry further suggests, "What can be said is that the foundations of a new historical period, the Ecozoic Era, have been established in every realm of human affairs." (Berry, 1999, p.201) It is an intensely challenging thought to recognize that I stand at a place in time where the importance of teaching respect and understanding of the Earth is crucial for my students and for the future of our world. As fossil fuel supplies diminish we have reached a point where recycling and the use of new technologies such as solar, and wind power are becoming no longer just novel ideas but areas that need to be avidly pursued.

In the book *EarthDance*, examples are given of some companies that are already choosing new directions: "Meanwhile, a few oil companies, such as Sunoco and BP-Amoco are taking steps toward the inevitable phase-out of the oil economy, investing in solar energy and other alternatives, requesting pollution taxes for the entire industry, etc." (Sahtouris, 2000, p. 357). As a teacher I make it a point to regularly find articles about alternative energy possibilities in current magazines to share with my students, as well as sharing my own experiences of living in a house completely powered by solar electricity. It is my goal that they have an understanding that this is a simple and feasible way to live in harmony with our environment. Other ideas for alternative energy and ecological sanity are suggested by Kiyo Matsumoto in this online posting:

> Biomass is a renewable energy resource derived from the carbonaceous waste of various human and natural activities. It is derived from numerous sources, including the by-products from the timber industry, agricultural crops, raw material from the forest, major parts of household waste and wood. ??Biomass does not add carbon dioxide to the atmosphere as it absorbs the same amount of carbon in growing as it releases when consumed as a fuel. Its advantage is that it can be used to generate

electricity with the same equipment or power plants that are now burning fossil fuels. Biomass is an important source of energy and the most important fuel worldwide after coal, oil and natural gas.

Traditional use of biomass is more than its use in modern application. In the developed world biomass is again becoming important for applications such as combined heat and power generation. In addition, biomass energy is gaining significance as a source of clean heat for domestic heating and community heating applications. In fact in countries like Finland, USA and Sweden the per capita biomass energy used is higher than it is in India, China or in Asia.
(edugreen.teri.res.in/explore/renew/renew.htm)

Composting is the transformation of organic material (plant matter) through decomposition into a soil-like material called compost. Invertebrates (insects and earthworms), and microorganisms (bacteria and fungi) help in transforming the material into compost. Composting is a natural form of recycling, which continually occurs in nature.

Today there are several different reasons why composting remains an invaluable practice. Yard and food wastes make up approximately 30% of the waste stream in the United States. Composting most of these waste streams would reduce the amount of Municipal Solid Waste (MSW) requiring disposal by almost one fourth, while at the same time provide a nutrient-rich soil amendment. Compost added to gardens improves soil structure, texture, aeration, and water retention. When mixed with compost, clay soils are lightened, and sandy soils retain water better. Mixing compost with soil also contributes to erosion control, soil fertility, proper pH balance, and healthy root development in plants.

(HowToCompost.org) (ties-edu.org/campus/HMC2 Capra, Sahtouris, & Montessori, integrative seminar, 4:86)

It is also important to me to share with my students how the use of petroleum products contributes to pollution, which has been linked to global warming. This global warming is especially alarming when considered as a social justice issue. The people most likely to be impacted by droughts and the resulting crop failures live in areas of the world where basic sustainability of life is already very difficult. It is vital that students understand that what each of us does really can help or hinder the other people that we share our planet with. When my students question why so many people in other parts of the world are angry with Americans, this is something I need to help them understand. As a nation we have been blessed with great resources, but that also means that we have great responsibilities to use those resources wisely for the benefit of our entire planet. I am deeply impressed by these words of Montessori's:

> When danger threatens a nation, all its citizens unite for defense, and many times the very threat of danger brings unity in a country previously split into hostile political or religious factions. The danger that threatens us today has perhaps been visited upon us by destiny in order that all humanity may unite for its common defense. (Montessori, 1949/1999, p.60)

Gang suggests that at this point in our history there are many thinkers who are encouraging and inspiring others to look at the necessary future changes:

> In general these "twenty-first century thinkers" explain that in the next twenty-five years there will be sweeping changes in all of our frames of reference. These will be triggered by the gradual shift from the mechanical-industrial age to the information-solar age. It will mark the transition away from a non-renewable energy base toward renewable sources of energy, from a period of super-specialization toward a time of holistic disciplines, and from a dichotomy between man and nature towards a unifying grasp of reality. (Gang, 1989, p.20)

There are also many other ways to live gently on the earth, and I think it is very important not to get overwhelmed by the enormity of the task. It is an inspiring thought to consider that each person doing even a few things will make a big difference. Harry Beudel gave these suggestions in an online posting:

> Finally I may have seemed pessimistic about changing the world but as I reflect I have been disappointed with how much we waste as a household, as a school, and as a society. I can directly control waste in my household, make suggestions at school, and most importantly be politically aware and VOTE. We cannot make excuses and blame our leaders. We put them there and need to replace them when they don't serve our best interests. (ties-edu.org/campus/HMC2 Capra, Sahtouris, and Montessori, integrative seminar, 4:91)

I am often amazed at how quickly our classroom can become disheveled, especially if we are working on a messy project together. However, just as we all participated in making the mess, it seems when we all play our role in cleaning up, it can just as easily become tidy again. In the book *The Web of Life*, Fritjof Capra expands on this concept:

> Instead of being a machine, nature at large turns out to be more like human nature-unpredictable, sensitive to the surrounding world, influenced by small fluctuations. Accordingly, the appropriate way of approaching nature to learn about her complexity and beauty is not through domination and control, but through respect, cooperation, and dialogue. (Capra, 1996, p. 193)

It is my hope that the more aware students are of all the gifts the universe has to offer, the more they will respect and honor their environment. The realization that they exist in a place of mutual respect with their environment will hopefully lead to a greater sense of their role in using natural resources wisely and being a part of creating technology which benefits both humans and the environment.

The concept of respect plays an enormous role in the growth I have experienced as a part of my training as a Montessori teacher. Respect for myself, the environment, and the relationships that I have with others, all join together to create a deeper sense of peace in my life. Respect for each of the students in my classroom is probably the most important part of the process of my understanding of how education impacts peace.

When presenting information to my students, I often think back to my training in Houston, where some information was presented very gently and I was able to eagerly grasp it, and other information was lost in translation. I think about what environments were prepared for me in a way that made information easy for me to grasp, and I try to teach in those ways. Some days I unintentionally slip into traditional dogma, and when things invariably go awry, I step back and reflect and see that I have not honored the child or myself. I now understand how observing makes a Montessori classroom distinct from traditional learning environments.

Moving away from an ego-centered reality to honoring the spirit of life within all living beings is radical education. In today's educational world the fear of lawsuits may drive teachers to be physically kinder to children, but the decision to honor the child because you give honor to all things is, unfortunately, still a very foreign concept. I now have a greater understanding and awareness that the ages from six to nine are sensitive periods of students for grasping their cosmic task, meaning their ideas of their place and purpose in the universe. The chance to honor their needs at the point in which they are in my classroom guides the way I prepare and present our classroom environment. Duffy and Duffy promote the idea of using Cosmic Education with students ranging in ages from six to nine to help them discover their cosmic task:

> This power of imagination and the ability to abstract from what they know concretely means that children are not limited in their search for knowledge-the universe itself is the limit. As part of Cosmic Education, Montessori believed that the intelligence and imaginative powers of children should stretch out into the farthest reaches of the universe in order to understand themselves as human beings and to discover their cosmic task. (Duffy & Duffy, 2002, p.9)

Val McAvey comments on the importance of teaching cosmic education during the early elementary years in an online posting:

> I agree this sense of wonder is the beginning of wisdom. It is so lovely to think about.
>
> Once again, Maria Montessori was way ahead of her time. How fortunate are the children who are allowed the freedom to find their cosmic task in a safe environment, at a time when they are not battered by their hormones and the influences of the world. The children who begin Montessori education in early childhood have a unique opportunity to enter adolescence with a firm understanding of their place in the cosmos. If not an understanding, at least they have grappled with the subject and are not dealing with it for the first time, along with the physiological changes of puberty and the psychological challenges of dating.
>
> (ties-edu.org/campus/HMC2 Swimme, Gang, integrative seminar, 3:73)

In another online posting, Catherine Beall reveals a personal experience with cosmic education:

> Another part of the book that hit home with me is summarized by the following quote:
>
> "A single surprising shudder passes through you and you realize you are standing on the back of something like a cosmic whale, one that is slowly rotating its great bulk on the surface of an unseen ocean…It is true that,

soon afterward, we snap right back into our everyday way of experiencing the world." (Swimme, 1999, pg.27)

I had this experience this past spring. I was driving home from school, late one evening. It was dark outside and it was one of those nights where the moon was full, clear, and enormous. I was on a stretch of Highway 98 that is not well lit or populated. I suddenly had this feeling of falling in the pit of my stomach as I realized and FELT that our planet was out in space with the millions of other heavenly bodies. I felt as though my car and I would suddenly float off the road and into space.

Overall, I am proud to be Montessorian, educating children with what we know of the universe and instilling in them a sense of awe and wonder about the universe and their place in it. This book has given me new insight into the universe that I look forward to passing along to my students. (ties-edu.org/campus/HMC2, Swimme, Gang, integrative seminar, 3:10)

I really treasure the idea of being part of a living movement of honoring others and leading them into a change in consciousness. This idea has not only guided a transformation of my teaching during the hours of eight to three, but also inspired a realization that every action and thought I have is an opportunity to teach and learn with others. The Lebanese writer, Kahlil Gibran expresses this same thought in the book, *The Prophet*:

> Your daily life is your temple and your religion.
> Whenever you enter into it take with you your all.

> Take the plough and the forge and the mallet and the lute,
>
> The things you have fashioned in necessity or for delight.
>
> For in reverie you cannot rise above your achievements
>
> nor fall lower that your failures.
>
> And take with you all men:
>
> For in adoration you cannot fly higher than their hopes nor humble
>
> yourself lower than their despair. (Gibran, 1923/1982, p.78)

This part of my transformation has been highly influenced by interacting with many people that I have encountered since entering my Montessori training. It amazes me to think of all the new friends I have made and the lessons I have learned as a result of this juncture of my life.

Influences of Other People

When one begins any new journey, one feels a sense of adventure-not only for the physical journey, but for the emotional journey as well. Many of these emotional places have occurred for me as a by-product of my encounters with the travelers that have crossed my path. Some of these have been people I have simply observed and learned from others have had a more intimate impact on my life. Our conversations and interactions have caused new parts of my personality to surface which I never realized existed.

There are so many people that have crossed my path: teachers at the Houston Montessori Center, students at the center, and parents at my school, other teachers at my school, my own students, and just random encounters with people who distilled for me ideas which seemed free-floating until they were personified. While this is a difficult subject to limit, there are several people that for one reason or another seem very pertinent to my transformation.

Elizabeth Coe, PhD, of the Houston Montessori Center had a profound affect on how I thought about peace. The Philosophy classes she taught and the conversations I had with her, opened up new pathways of understanding that peace is a personal responsibility. Peace should never be considered the easy path. An important lesson I learned from her is that peace requires a willingness to look within and soul search for any attitudes that may be a barrier to peaceful relationships. Diamond discusses the idea that conflict can be a good experience in *The Peace Book*:

> Conflict is a normal part of human interaction. It can even be a positive experience, because it gives us the opportunity to grow greater love, kindness, and compassion in our relationships. It also helps us learn how to solve problems effectively. (Diamond, 2002, p.121)

It is necessary to do the hard work of changing those characteristics within me in order to value the relationship more than getting my own way. It is critical that I am willing to look at my own hidden motives or fears that might be hindering the relationship. Our conversations led to ideas about being at peace within oneself in order to share peace with others, and the recognition that no matter how strongly you feel about peace and try to create peace within your relationships, other people still have the right to reject it. There is a fine line between motivating others to be peaceful and manipulating them into peace. I think that in traditional education, it is common to threaten students or bribe them into being peaceful. In the book *Next of Kin*, Roger Fouts writes, "When a relationship is not built on mutual respect, the only way of maintaining control is through brutal force." (Fouts, 1997, p.140) It is a very different approach to walk a path of peace and invite students to join the journey and to discover the sights together.

One event that really captivated my thoughts was the opportunity to hear Nobel Peace Prize winner Jody Williams speak on the subject of, "The Power of One" at a lecture that she gave at the University of Tennessee in Martin on November 8, 2004. It seemed very synchronistic as the study of Nobel Peace Prize winners was also the subject of my research project for my Montessori training. I embrace the concepts of "The Power of One", because sometimes it can be overwhelming to look at a whole system. You wonder where to even start in order to make a difference. I am beginning to understand that the key is to start with yourself and let the power of being a positive influence take over. Williams reminded the audience of the importance of just choosing something to be passionate about in order to change the world. Her practical personality, combined with her earnestness and compassion, was both deeply touching and thought provoking.

This was a woman who could have easily spent the night talking about what she had accomplished, but instead chose to motivate her audience to think about what they could accomplish, and how that accomplishment could transform the world into a better place.

That message really touched my heart and made me look at how the things I pour my time and energy into matter on a grander scheme. It made me realize even more deeply the importance of my job and the impact I have on my students. Working in a Montessori environment allows me the opportunity to join with colleagues who are sending out a message to the world that peace is possible. In her book, *Leadership and the New Science*, Wheatley affirms the importance of sending out a consistent concept in which we believe:

> Now we need to imagine ourselves as beacon towers of information, standing tall in the integrity of what we say, pulsing out congruent messages everywhere. We need all of us out there, stating, clarifying, reflecting, modeling, filling all of space with the messages we care about. If we do that a powerful field develops-and with it, the wondrous capacity to organize into coherent, capable form. (Wheatley, 1999, p.57)

It encourages me a great deal to know that often when visitors come to our school they are given the opportunity to see how beautiful a peaceful environment can be. We have an organization in my community called, "Leadership Jackson." This organization takes leaders of business and civic organizations and gives them the opportunity to tour and get to know many different aspects of our community. Since my classroom is at the end of the hallway of our school, and my class is often at lunch when they tour, I have had several opportunities to talk with these visiting leaders. I think it is very interesting that even though we have the oldest school building in Jackson and are woefully lacking in technology, these leaders are extremely impressed with our environment. It has been delightful for me to talk with them and guide them to an understanding of the culture of respect that precedes our peaceful environment. I encourage them to remember that whether dealing with children or adults, in every situation a choice can be made for peace, and that peace has its roots in respect. When I explain how we work through conflicts using the Peace Bear ceremony they are amazed at the simplicity of it and they often realize this same approach could be used for conflict resolution in their own jobs.

One of the valuable friendships I developed during my training was with another student at the Houston Montessori Center, Val McAvey. McAvey sat next to me during class. As we shared colored pencils and life stories, my respect for her grew daily. One of the many lessons I learned from McAvey is that time is indeed relative. When considering the people in our lives, we should always look at time as very short. Having lost several people close to her in a one-year period, she placed great importance on the relationships in her life. If I had a problem, she was willing to take the time away from her long "to do" list and listen to me. I watched closely as she interacted with the other people in her life over and over. For the most part, when she took the time to do this, the things on her list were eventually accomplished, and time seemed to expand to allow her to do that. As I watched this occur over the summer, I thought about how often I probably had my priorities mixed up and put the "to do" list in front of the people in my life. In the Montessori classroom, this seems to show up every day, and it always amazes me how taking the time to honor students where they are and give them a few moments of emotional safety allows lessons to proceed with greater effectiveness. Wheatley describes the effect acting locally can have on our world:

> The fall of the Berlin Wall demonstrates the power of "think globally, act locally." It proves that local actions can have enormous influence on a monstrous system that had resisted all other political attempts to change it. Germany could not be reunified by traditional power politics, or by high-level leaders from powerful nations. It was local actions within the system, combined with many other influences globally, that coalesced into a moment of profound change. (Wheatley, 1999, p.44)

It thrills me to think that my action of choosing to treat others around me, especially my students, with respect and honor might have profound implications for the world. In listening to them, I feel that I am validating their lives, and in truth they are validating mine also. Our communication together is starting a conversation of respect and peace that can be overheard by people all over the world. It is a conversation that is carried home to parents, to future spouses, to future children, to business relationships, to friendships, and to a wide world that is longing for this evolution of peace and respect to occur.

One of the other things McAvey did was introduce me to a place in Houston called Mercy Street. Mercy Street is an outreach of the church McAvey attends. It is a gathering of a wide cross section of people on Saturday night. At this gathering, you will find a great range of races and beliefs: drug addicts, alcoholics, prostitutes, professors, wealthy businessmen, religious leaders, and the average Houstonian gathered together in order to look for hope outside of themselves. It is an avenue for reaching out to help one another. Mercy Street had a profound impact on me because I was able to see, in action, all the radical ideas I was learning in Montessori training. These ideas include honoring one another no matter how different we may seem, and finding a purpose and place in the world. It was a microcosm of what I was coming to believe could occur in the entire world. To see it in reality gave me an intense longing to see that type of understanding and respect on a larger scale. In the book, *Being Peace,* Thich Nhat Hanh comments on how our perceptions impact our world:

> Suppose while walking in the twilight, you see a snake, and you scream, but when you shine your flashlight on it, it turns out to be a rope. This is an error of perception. During our daily lives we have many misperceptions. If I don't understand you, I may be angry all the time. We are not capable of understanding each other, and that is the main source of human suffering. (Nhat Hanh, 1987/2005, p. 41)

The salient memory of my experience with the group that met at Mercy Street was that someone was willing to say that everyone deserves respect, no matter where they may be in their lives. From that point, they provided a place for many different people to come together to get to know each other better, thus shattering many negative misconceptions. The environment that was created for them was one of honesty and respect. It allowed each person the opportunity to be exactly who they authentically were, with the knowledge that they would be honored just for being there, even if they were different in personality and experiences. This atmosphere provided a new way of experiencing the world and allowed many misperceptions to slip away. I realized that this same type of respectful atmosphere is being created in Montessori schools all over the country.

When I returned from training and started my first full year of teaching at a Montessori school, there were many people that helped to guide me. One of those was the curriculum coordinator at our school, Melinda Harris. Harris has a wonderful way of talking with people. She is gentle yet firm, assertive but always respectful. From her example, I learned about the importance of self-control. When talking with students, even very difficult students, her sagacious personality always gave them opportunities to preserve their dignity. Grace and courtesy are important words at my school, and I feel like Harris was probably my best teacher to help me discover what those words really meant, especially when speaking with other people. It is very easy for me to get caught up in my own agenda instead of really observing and listening to other people. Harris is very good at practicing dialogue as opposed to just having discussions. I have come to treasure her wisdom which mirrors these thoughts by Jiddu Krishnamurti from his book, *Education and the Significance of Life.*

> To have an open mind is more important than learning; and we can have an open mind, not by cramming it full of information, but by being aware of our own thoughts and feelings, by carefully observing ourselves and the influences about us, by listening to others, by watching the rich and the poor, the powerful and the lowly. Wisdom does not come through fear and oppression, but through the observation and understanding of everyday incidents in human relationship. (Krishnamurti, 1981, p.64)

Observing others with an open mind relieves me of many preconceptions which may be wrong and damaging to an atmosphere of peace. I am often amazed at the new perspectives gained when listening to students during circle time sharing their concerns and acknowledgements that I might not have seen on my own.

Two people Harris brought in for special inservice meetings were Marilyn Eblen and Teri Canaday. Eblen is the mother of one of my students; she also has a background in working with deaf students. Eblen gave an inservice on using sign language in the classroom. Sign language has been a wonderful tool, allowing quieter transitions, and increasing the observation powers of my students. Using sign language to talk to a student across the room has increased grace and courtesy in our room by providing a quieter atmosphere. As a part of my TIES course work, I read the book, *Next of Kin* by Roger Fouts. This book was the story of Fouts developing relationships with chimpanzees that had been taught American Sign Language.

> Clearly chimpanzees are capable of intellectual feats that once we thought unique to humans. Not only can they reason, plan for the immediate future, and solve simple problems, but their proficiency in ASL shows that they can understand and use abstract symbols in their communication. Washoe was even able to pass on this skill to her adopted son. (Fouts, 1997, p.x)

Since sign language is used daily in our classroom, I was very interested in it being used as a form of communication between species. Respect and communication formed an important link to create better understanding between Fouts and Washoe. I can see that sign language performs the same task in our classroom. My students were very interested when I shared the story of Fouts and Washoe. It was a story which struck their imaginations and sparked lively conversation about what it would be like to have the opportunity to communicate with a member of another species. It is my hope that conversations like this further enhance the idea for my students that we have a lot to learn from the creatures that share our planet.

Teri Canaday is the owner of a private Montessori school in town. Harris arranged for Canaday to give an inservice on positive discipline. For me, one of the most meaningful ideas from this inservice was using "I feel statements" when dealing with problems between a student and myself. My students had already been using "I feel statements" on a daily basis when using the Peace Bear if a conflict came up between them. I had never thought about the idea that I could use "I feel statements" when I was having an issue with a student. Now, I frequently use these statements to clarify what I am observing. For instance, I may say, "I feel concerned when I see you are not working on your contract because I wonder if you do not know what to do, or if something is bothering you." Then I might add, "I would like for you to tell me why you are not working on your contract." This has given me many new insights; one of those was that I had not done a complete job of discussing with my students why working on their contract was important. Using "I feel statements" is a valuable way to stop and think about what feelings are occurring, and how they might be affecting us. In her book, *Shining Through*, Sonnie McFarland describes the importance of distinguishing our feelings from who we are.

> Our emotions are always fluctuating, and we often identify who we are by them, i.e., "I am angry!" rather than "I feel angry." Emotions are indicators of our feelings, but do not determine who we are. They are extremely powerful, and without proper understanding of them we allow them to control our body, mind and spirit. Learning to be aware of our emotions and how to handle them effectively increases our ability to stay centered and in touch with our true spiritual nature. (McFarland, 1993, p.17)

This idea that emotions are fluid and changeable is a valuable concept for students to understand in order to promote peace in the environment. It can be very freeing for anyone to admit and honor their feelings rather than feeling controlled by them. Honoring feelings provides a way to bring about inner respect and peace.

Recently my students and I had a circle time discussion about anger. I wanted to talk about this topic because one of the students was having angry outbursts on a regular basis. As I began the conversation, one of the students kept ignoring me and was making a scene rather than listening to what I had to say. I started to become very angry, and my students saw my frustration. I quickly realized what was happening and started laughing at myself because I was providing a perfect example of what I wanted to discuss. I used the situation to question what was happening with my emotions. The students easily identified that anger was the secondary emotion that I was feeling. With extreme accuracy, they explained that under my anger, I was feeling embarrassed, frustrated, disappointed, disrespected, and hurt by his ignoring me. We then talked about the choices that can be made when these emotions surface. Since I respected my student and realized that he was probably just feeling excited and ready for lunch, it was easy for me to recognize that while my feelings were valid, they didn't need to be acted upon in such a strong way. I was able to use the Peace Bear conflict approach and ask my student if he was willing to be patient for a few more minutes until it was time to leave for lunch. This experience not only offered a wonderful real life example of dealing with feelings, it also impressed on my heart how wise and articulate children are when they are given the opportunity to speak from their hearts. It seems to me that the students in my classroom are willing to offer their wisdom freely to me because I am willing to listen and think deeply about their thoughts, and I am willing to be real with them. In an online posting Kiyo Matsumoto shared these thoughts about listening to children:

There are many things I have been learning and discovering through these readings. While I am working on my research, I had an interview with two students the other day. As I learned from "Active Interview" and Bohm's "On Dialogue", I prepared myself not becoming to be a leader of the conversation. I really had to work hard to make myself listen to what they had to say. Through the interview what I learned was that it is so important for children to have this kind of opportunities where they can feel and experience that what they say is valuable and people respectfully listen to them. I think that children will learn to have the kind of dialogue Bohm suggests if we keep providing enough opportunities and appropriate environment. It seems to me that our tendency of trying to "win" over the conversation is a result of years of negative experiences of not being heard. (ties-edu.org/campus/HMC2, Bohm, Peat-Briggs integrative seminar, 1:7)

While Harry Buedel shared his experience of working with adolescents:

When I did my research regarding adolescents experiencing Montessori for the first time they often remarked about how surprised they were that they had opportunities to talk. They were conditioned that the teacher talks and the student listens. One of my subjects stated in so many words that our class was different because teachers don't talk all the time, many times they listen, and the teachers care about what is being said. I felt that was a great compliment, even though the student probably was aware it was. (ties-edu.org/campus/HMC2 Bohm, Peat-Briggs integrative seminar, 1:117)

In her book, *Nurturing the Spirit,* Wolf offers her thoughts on the need for teachers to be real with students:

> In order to hide our shadow side from others, most of us wear an invisible mask. The mask is not our true self but is the way we want others to see us. Teachers often wear the mask of perfection, never wanting to admit a weakness to their students, when actually talking about their own flaws would make them more accessible. (Wolf, 1996, p.35)

There is true freedom in that statement, freedom for both the teacher and the student. What a burden it seems to release the heart of the child to recognize that perfection is something to strive for, but not a fault if it is not reached. Our mistakes are opportunities for us to learn and discover how to do something differently the next time, not something for us to be afraid of. Dorrie Pearson had this to say regarding making mistakes:

> I believe it is important for the children to see all members of our community as learners, as well as a community that can learn from its mistakes and accomplishments, in hopes that they will be inspired to learn all of their lives. (ties-edu.org/campus/HMC2 Capra, Sahtouris, and Montessori, integrative seminar, 4:27)

A student in this type of open environment is given the opportunity to be real rather than being stunted in their emotional growth. Wolf reflects on this environment:

> Montessori had ingeniously provided an environment that, instead of adding spiritual essence to the child's nature, had revealed what was already there. Somehow this spirit had been blocked in other educational situations. Children behaved badly because they lived in conditions in which their spirituality could not express itself. Their spirits rebelled in violence, withdrawal, selfishness and disregard for others. After several months Montessori was truly astonished as she saw these negative characteristics gradually recede in the children in her Casa dei Bambini. At that point she recognized for the first time the true spirit within the child. What was remarkable was that the children themselves had helped her to see this. (Wolf, 1996, p.28)

Another positive role model at my school was Taja Sanders, a teacher down the hall from me. Sanders has taught in several Montessori schools, but never in a traditional school, so her insights come from only having a Montessori background. One of the gifts that I received from Sanders was how beautiful and meaningful "strike-the-imagination" stories can be. Sanders is able to find amazing metaphors to reach into the hearts and lives of her children. She has very high expectations for her students, but she also uses story as a way to help them see how they can accomplish those expectations. I felt like every time I walked into her room I learned something new and helpful. One of those times was the day a student had finished working on something very difficult, and Sanders just smiled at him and asked him how he felt about his work, and he replied,

"Accomplished". This struck me so powerfully. Knowing Sanders, I am sure she had given a motivational speech at some point to her students about how wonderful accomplishing your goals can feel. When I saw the look on this student's face and his pride at working through a difficult task, it was a significant paradigm shift for me of how important it is to empower students to be able to take initiative and work on their own. This idea applies not only to working through academic issues but also relationship issues. Donna Bryant Goertz addresses this idea in an example she gives in her book, *Children Who Are Not Yet Peaceful*, about a young man who was redirected during circle time to find a peaceful solution to conflict.

> "Peter, you're smart enough and fine enough to figure out a better way to handle Malcolm's irritating behavior. Children, this is Peter's work, to choose nonviolent solutions, and all of us must support him. Peter has great passion, and he will begin to direct it to help others. Right now he's faking power by hitting anyone in his path. He's scared, so he strikes out to hurt, but he's here with us in our community to grow out of that. Our work is to know he can do it and to look for every sign of progress."
>
> (Goertz, 2001, p.144)

This conversation that Goertz has with her students is a really good example of how we co-create our universe through what we choose to give our attention to and notice. Wheatley discusses this idea of both the individual and the system working together to produce a present reality:

> For years I had struggled conceptually with a question I thought important: In organizations, which is the more important influence on

behavior-the system or the individual? The quantum world answered that question for me with a resounding, "Both." There are not either/ors. There is no need to decide between two things, pretending they are separate. What is critical is the relationship created between two or more elements. Systems influence individuals, and individuals call forth systems. It is the relationship that evokes the present reality. Which potential becomes real depends on the people, the events, and the moment." (Wheatley, 1999, p.36)

I am very impressed that Goertz encouraged her students to choose as a work noticing when Peter was successful at reaching his goal. Community offers an opportunity to reinforce positive visions. As Gang aptly states, "Clearly, it is not possible to observe reality without changing it. The participation of the observer alters the result. In human terms, it means that each person "counts" and has the ability to effect other people and events." (Gang, 1989, p.34) What a motivating idea it is to realize that it can be our work as a global community to notice and encourage peace, to know that it is a work that we can accomplish together as we join together to look for non-violent solutions.

Another characteristic in my friend Taja Sanders I have grown to love and respect is her constant soul searching to be the best person she can be. This idea of soul searching seems to have been an often-repeated component of my Montessori experience. Reflecting often, especially as a result of my TIES course work, was a prominent part of the transformation occurring within me. I became a social scientist always observing what things seemed to work and looking for new pathways when things seemed dysfunctional. I discovered that if I have a problem with a child not showing respect towards me, the best thing for me to do is to find a quiet spot and center myself; once I have "re-membered" this sense of my own self worth, it is much easier for me to relate to and respect the student so that they have a reason to respect me. It seems to me that the reason adults often have a difficult time honoring children is because they have never discovered their own sense of self worth, and without being able to value themselves, it is impossible for them to value children. In his book, *The Hidden Messages of Water*, Masaru Emoto reflects on the concept that outer experiences are seemingly drawn into our lives due to our inner choices and attitudes.

> If you fill your heart with love and gratitude, you will find yourself surrounded by so much that you can love and that you can feel grateful for, and you can even get closer to enjoying the life of health and happiness that you seek. But what will happen if you emit signals of hate, dissatisfaction, and sadness? Then you will probably find yourself in a situation that makes you hateful, dissatisfied, and sad. (Emoto, 2004, p.52)

This has been a very good admonition for me to remember. It is my belief that it is very important for me to keep my own thoughts on a higher level in order to have a positive effect on my students and on the world. If I am constantly taking the time to reflect on my life, it is an easier task to see when things have become off balance in order for me to return to a state of inner harmony.

One of the ways I reflected and felt the need to change was regarding the way I give lessons. I really struggled, and still struggle, with all the many expectations that occur as a result of teaching in a public school. I am still not sure what to do with all the workbooks residing in my classroom. It has been a tremendous challenge to teach three grade levels and to know how to use the resources the school board provides and expects teachers to use, with all the lessons and materials also expected of a Montessori school. Somewhere along the middle of my first year, I decided I had to make a conscious decision about where to place my emphasis. It was a powerful choice to commit to trusting the Montessori materials. Once that decision was made, things became much simpler for me. I still found ways to use the workbooks, but my heart had made an indispensable leap that proved to be the right choice for me. This decision allowed me to be more confident and relaxed because I realized that if I didn't cover everything in the school board provided workbooks, the students would still learn what they needed to learn and even more.

In his book, *The Montessori Controversy*, Chattin-McNichols comments on this idea of the Montessori teacher trusting the materials and the child.

> The Montessori teacher has a great deal of faith in the child, and in what he will learn through interacting with the Montessori materials that he chooses himself. The goal of the teacher's work is to provide an environment where this concentration can exist. Respect for the child should guide the teacher in doing this. (Chattin-McNichols, 1998, P.66)

There was one student in particular that really taught me about how this occurs. While an intelligent student, Mandy is not very persistent, and if I didn't give a lesson clearly enough she would walk away and never bother to touch that material again without tremendous prodding. She inadvertently taught me the importance of slowing down and watching closely to make sure what I am saying is connecting with the student.

The other lesson I learned from Mandy was about really caring and loving difficult people. While all of us struggled with how to relate to the special classmate that hit, bit, screamed and pouted when she didn't get her way, Mandy went out of her way every day to be kind and helpful to this student. Mandy's mother related conversations at home that revealed the depth of concern she felt about her classmate's social behavior. She often prayed for her and really thought about the best ways to interact with her. She was a beautiful example of how to love the spirit within someone even if their behavior is unacceptable. The Dalai Lama offers this response to the question of how to love someone that has caused you great suffering:

> In 1959 Mao Tse-tung's Communist troops killed thousands of my countrymen and occupied the whole nation. I myself fled across the Himalayan mountains into neighboring India, where I have lived in exile ever since. The Tibetan people, therefore, have every reason to hate the Chinese for the unimaginable suffering they caused our people. But whenever such feelings arise in us, we turn inward. We try to develop compassion for the Chinese, too. An enemy remains a person, no matter what he or she has done. As an individual, as a human being, he continues to deserve our respect and our love. We do however condemn his ill-intended acts. If necessary, we also have to protect ourselves from them.
> (Stiekel, 2003, p.67)

Mandy and the Dalai Lama both share the idea that respect is the beginning of change in a relationship with someone that has made negative or violent choices. The internal strength of peace reaches out to an enemy without fear. What a beautiful, transformative concept. Each of us, through the power of respect, can clearly set boundaries of what is acceptable and what is not acceptable. Being a peacemaker does not mean that you have to degrade yourself in order to keep peace, for that type of peace becomes violence against your own soul. Montessori states, "The real danger threatening humanity is the emptiness in men's souls; all the rest is merely a consequence of this emptiness." (Montessori, 1949/1999, p.46) It makes sense to me that any time I degrade myself; I am losing sight of my purpose and reason for being a part of the universe. This adds to the emptiness of my soul, and is a loss of opportunity to contribute to peace in the world.

Other Experiences

A part of my transformation has come from the opportunity to reflect about my life through verbal or online conversations with others about my Montessori experiences. I often found myself sending out long e-mails detailing some new idea I had run across through my course work. It was fun to share these insights with others and to hear their responses. Some were very thought provoking, and some were very challenging to encourage me to dig deeper and learn even more. I received several suggestions for books or movies that might be helpful to me. After reading "The Seven Lessons of Chaos" by Briggs and Peat, I became even more interested in quantum theory and managed to sneak in several books off the required reading list that detailed more about these ideas. I also watched several popular movies, including the current movies titled, *What the Bleep?* (Goldwyn, 2004) and *The Elegant Universe* (Nova & Greene, 2003). These movies seemed to engage in similar concepts.

An online posting further reveals my interest in quantum subjects:

> Allison, I agree that Phil's book is a refreshing look at how we model education; our enthusiasm and determination to teach the interdependence of all subjects are needed in the classroom and in teacher education courses. For me personally though, the physics sections were major bifurcation points in which I suddenly wanted to absorb everything I could on the subject. It fascinated me that our thoughts literally change what is happening around us and have a butterfly effect around the world.
>
> (ties-edu.org/campus/HMC2 Swimme, Gang, integrative seminar, 3:89)

When I mentioned this new fascination for quantum theory to several friends they all said that I should talk to Kenny Jones. Jones has been a friend to our family for twelve years, and unfortunately for us, recently accepted a new job to teach art at a university in a different state. I had a real concern that the frenetic pace of his family moving would never allow us the opportunity to discuss these ideas in great detail. I was very blessed however, and two nights before he left, we had the opportunity to sit down and have a long conversation about both quantum and string theory and their relevance to our lives. I believe that as we fish back through the memories of our lives, there are pockets of time we are able to sink deeply into, and pull out rich wealth. That night and that conversation will always be a deep pocket of understanding for me. Jones was able to explain some of the pertinent ideas about quantum theory to me in a very simple fashion which, unbeknownst to him, built on everything I had been reading over the past six months. The idea that atomic particles could have a duality of existence that seemed to respond and take their shape from the expectations of the person observing them was fascinating to me from both a scientific and relational perspective. I kept repeating, "Yes, yes, it all makes sense," while he looked amazed that I understood what he was talking about. I thought of this moment later when I read Wheatley's words in *Leadership and the New Science*:

> I find pleasure in letting these new ideas swirl freely inside me. Like clouds, they begin as mist, then take form, then dissipate. Clouds themselves are self organizing, taking new shape as thunderstorms, hurricanes, or rain fronts depending on changes in their environment. We are capable of similar transformations; new ideas can emerge as powerful insights if we allow them the freedom to self-organize. And there is much we can learn from clouds. They are spectacular examples of fluid and responsive systems, structured in ways we never imagined possible: "After all, how do you hold a hundred tons of water in the air with no visible means of support? You build a cloud. (Wheatley, 1999, p.90)

As I try to decipher why this experience was so crucial for me, I think it had something to do with feeling closer to a cosmic destiny. It gave me a deeper understanding of the universe around me and how I participate in helping to transform the world around me through positive thoughts and energy. In my opinion, it related back to the speech that Nobel Peace Prize winner Jody Williams presented on "the power of one". It also connected with the lessons I had learned about the importance of first creating peace within myself.

One experience I had over the summer which allowed me to reach deeply and create peace within was an unexpected vacation to a small resort on Smith Lake in middle Tennessee. One afternoon, I sat by this placid lake and thought deeply about my first year of teaching in a Montessori school, especially about my experiences with the student that had so many social struggles. I took the time to sit still and feel any emotions that had been bottled up as a result of the experience.

I recognized where I felt those emotions in my body, and instead of fighting against them, I just experienced them. This, in some unexplainable way, allowed me the opportunity to accept them, accept myself, and accept everyone involved, and then to let go. This created a beautiful metamorphosis of the experience from pain and struggle, to learning and forgiveness. It made me think about how I forfeit inner peace when I don't take the time or emotional energy to completely struggle through my inner conflicts.

Perspective Changes

The training and experiences I went through during my first year of teaching in a Montessori school presented many different view points for me to ponder which resulted in several changes in my perceptions about teaching. One of the most crucial is the understanding of how important my job is. While I always felt being a teacher was a noble calling, I have come to a sense of urgency that I didn't feel before. I have a special place, not just because I am a teacher, but because I am a Montessori teacher. My training and influence is not only more specialized, but it also makes me more difficult to replace. This perspective has come about for several reasons. I realized how hard it had been on my third graders to have a different teacher every year, and all three being new or untrained Montessori teachers. I can see how much harder everything was for them as opposed to my third-graders this year who have had a little more stability. I can see that having a three-year cycle with the same teacher is a real benefit, and the relationships that are formed are beneficial in helping a student to have a good start, instead of wasting so much time at the beginning of a year getting to know each other. The other reason this perspective shift occurred was from the experience of trying to train a new assistant, and getting used to a new principal who does not yet have Montessori training. Now that I have to stop and explain Montessori concepts to others, I realize how many of them I have completely assimilated. It makes me realize how much time and energy would be lost if I changed positions and someone else had to come in and take my place. An example of this occurred when I was in another teacher's room, and we noticed someone had put the light green subtraction drill cards behind the dark green cards. She made a sarcastic remark to me saying, "Yes, that is exactly where the light green cards belong." Then we started laughing and realized that an untrained Montessori teacher or assistant could have stared at those cards for a year and never been bothered, but it immediately captured our attention and had to be corrected. We understood from our training at the Houston Montessori Center that task cards in the math area that have been purchased from HMC are color-coded so that answers that do not require the exchange of numbers are printed on a lighter color of card stock than ones that require students to have knowledge of how to exchange. This means that the first subtraction task cards a student works with will be cards that are printed on the light green card stock.

  Another perspective change that occurred has been my realization of how much students can learn through the Montessori environment. When I first walked into a Montessori classroom, I was amazed to see works on the shelf that I did not even begin to understand. Now, I do not even think twice when a parent balks when they find out we are studying multiplication and division in the first grade. The materials isolate the difficulty, allowing students the chance to concentrate on only one idea at a time. These ideas also build upon one another, which allow the students to rapidly grasp difficult concepts.

One change I really love is an understanding that I am no longer just teaching students; rather, I am observing them teach themselves. It is a joy to see their faces when they understand a concept. I realize understanding came as a result of the students working through the materials and discovering the information they needed on their own. There is a wonderful story about Alexander the Great visiting the great thinker, Diogenes. Alexander asked Diogenes if there was anything he could do for him. Diogenes replied, "Only stand out of my light." As a Montessori teacher, I am constantly reminding myself to trust the materials and stay out of my students' light. When a student comprehends a concept, I know that they have made that information their own and not just memorized it for a test.

I also no longer feel I have to be the person with all of the power in the classroom. When there is an issue, we are able to openly discuss it and come up with solutions together. I have discussed with my students that our classroom is an example of a microcosm of the world, and while there are plenty of some things in our classroom, like pencils, there are other resources, like the checkerboard game that we have to figure out how to share. Then we discussed how we share world resources and our responsibility to make conscious decisions to care about all the people sharing our planet just like we care about the people sharing our classroom. It was very touching to hear these young students discuss ideas for how to make the world a better place and realize how awareness at a young age can transform the future. The skills they are learning as mediators and mentors will touch everyone they encounter.

In my opinion, Montessori is a system-based teaching method. There is an emphasis placed on the interdependence of all things, whether it is world natural resources, or looking at a child feeling sad and not being able to do very many works because something negative is happening at home. This is a very different approach than the "everyone turns to page 52 and complete it for a grade" mindset of my traditional teaching experience. This causes me to be more observant and challenges me to pull different aspects of all our lives together. An example of this occurred when I was giving an angle Geometry lesson to my third-grade students and I told them when I was a child, my parents and I went to old cemeteries to read the headstones. Due to the fact that some of the people that made the headstones could not spell well, they wrote, "She has gone to be with the angles." My students thought this was really funny. Later in the day, one of my third-graders came and told me that it was her brother's birthday. I almost started crying remembering the year before when her baby brother was born and then died after one short week of life. I looked at her and winked and said, "Do you think the angles are having a geometric birthday party for him?" She grinned and gave me a big hug. In a Montessori classroom, where everyone and everything is woven together and we have the time to have long term experiences together, life just seems more real and meaningful to me.

A perspective change that I feel affected not only me, but also many of the teachers with whom I trained, was the understanding that how we respond to any child has the potential to make an enormous impact on their life. I believe people are attracted to the teaching field because they want to make a difference, and yet there is still an "I am the boss" mentality. It is a real shift in perspective to look at every person and child and see them as your equal and to work together to make good choices for everyone instead of manipulating others into doing what you want them to do. Krishnamurti comments on this perspective change in the book *Education and the Significance of Life*.

> The true teacher is inwardly rich and therefore asks nothing for himself; he is not ambitious and seeks no power in any form; he does not use teaching as a means of acquiring position or authority, and therefore he is free from the compulsion of society and the control of governments. Such teachers have the primary place in an enlightened civilization, for true culture is founded, not on the engineers and technicians, but on the educators.
> (Krishnamurti, 1953/1981, p.97)

This attitude took a very real and concentrated effort at first because it required moving out of my own ego to see through the eyes of others, and sometimes it is still difficult, but a year of experiences has allowed me to see the benefits from this perspective shift. I have found, in most instances, the results have been far greater than if I had simply bullied my way through my own agenda.

Impacting Others

One of the many joys of being a Montessori teacher is the opportunity to have an impact not only on my students but also, due to the three year cycle of the curriculum, there is an opportunity to connect with parents in a more meaningful way. It has been a personal goal of mine to foster a strong sense of community between the parents. I have provided several opportunities for parents to get to know each other better and have some shared experiences to talk about with one another. I held a picnic at the beginning of the school year and the parents participated in some get-acquainted exercises. One of these activities involved introducing themselves and acting out something that they enjoyed doing. After introducing themselves they then went through and gave the name and acted out the activity of each person previously introduced. Even now, when someone from that picnic wants to refer to Donna's mother I find them saying something like, "You know, the woman who likes to play with babies." while cradling their arms back and forth in a rocking motion.

One of the projects that my students did at the beginning of the year was to create a classroom scrapbook with each of them working with their parents to make a page telling about their family. The scrapbook is now available for students to check out of the classroom and look at with their parents. This has provided a way for students to learn about each other's talents and lives outside of the school day and for parents to have a deeper sense of connection with their child's classmates and their families.

When we studied Nobel Peace Prize winners, our class had a special night for families to watch the students make their presentations. After the presentations were over, families stayed around, enjoyed snacks, and complimented each other on what a great job the kids had done. At the end of the year, at our school's wrap-up night I held a community meeting with everyone in the circle, sitting down on the floor, and had a sharing time for the parents to discuss what they had enjoyed the most about the year. Many of them talked about the presentations the students had done about the Nobel Peace Prize winners. This was touching to me for several reasons-one being that it was wonderful to hear the project we had all worked so hard on had impacted the parents so deeply, and the other to hear them openly sharing with one another as if they were all old friends. This is especially meaningful because our school is a magnet school drawing students from all over the county. I knew our classroom was opening the door for better relationships between students of different races and socioeconomic levels for the future, but now I was seeing close relationships occurring between the parents. To know I could be a part of this kind of impact in our society is personally very significant to me.

When I taught in a traditional setting, I had parents who would hardly even show up for a parent teacher conference. Trying to find a room parent was always a struggle. These parents seemed to feel very uncomfortable in the school setting. It is very telling to me that not only do the parents of my Montessori students stay in contact on a regular basis, but they often come into the classroom to volunteer and help with the students. They seem to find real joy in being in our class and often comment on the peaceful atmosphere and happy colors in our room. On Mother's Day, I sent out cards to all of my students' mothers to wish them a nice day and thank them for the job they do, which makes my job so enjoyable. One mother came to me afterwards and told me she kept the card in her purse so she could show it to other people. As a mother myself, I realize how much time and energy moms put into their family relationships and how much we all need encouragement that we are on the right path and what we are doing matters. It delighted me to know I had been able to encourage this mom so much. I believe one of the reasons that card had encouraged her, was because the Montessori environment nourishes deeper relationships between parents and teachers.

An interesting experience I had during the past year came as a result of doing an active interview with my principal as a part of my graduate course work. The interview in itself was enjoyable and thought provoking as we discussed ideas about inner and world peace. Later in the year, I was asked to speak at a large birthday party that was held for our principal. I used the notes I had taken as a part of the active interview to share some insights about our principal. Since the evening had been very light hearted, I was a little amazed to look into the faces of the audience and see how touched they were by my speech. Many of them were crying. This reaction made me understand once again how important the message of peace is and how crucial one person with a vision can be. It seems this is a pertinent message that has become a very core part of my life since my Montessori journey began.

Themes of Transformation

Along with an awareness that peace is an inner decision, a personal responsibility, and a concept I want to model for my students and others, there have been several other themes that have surfaced during the past two years since I became associated with the Montessori school. These themes have run consistently through the training experience I had during my time at the Houston Montessori Center, through my graduate studies with the TIES program, and through my time in my classroom. They have even found their way into friendships, outside activities, and outside readings during this time. When I look at these themes together, I can understand better the transformation in my attitude from working at the Montessori school, to knowing, now and for the rest of my life, I will consider myself, "A Montessori Teacher".

When I try to explain this concept to others I will always realize it is more than knowing the light green subtraction cards go in front of the dark green subtraction cards. When my assistant asks me how I can be so patient when redirecting a very hyperactive first grade student, I will think about chaos theory, and I will know this student is playing their role in our universe and how I respond to them is part of my role in the universe. I will know how I respond to my students will be crucial to how they feel about themselves, and others will pick up on my cues to know how to respond also. I will know my small steps of kindness have the power of butterfly wings and I may never know the blessings I am sending out into the world, but nevertheless their power will be felt.

When a student comes to me and asks if we can talk about a topic during our classroom meeting time, I now know to make time for that topic, as it may be far more important than my own agenda. It may even be a *bifurcation point*. Bifurcation is from the Latin word *bifurcus*, meaning two-forked, indicating a time of change. This change in the agenda sometimes opens a whole new level of understanding for my students. I understand in a clearer way, time is the most important resource in my classroom, and while I need to move my students through their lessons, the time I spend just listening to their thoughts may be the best use of time there is.

The relativity of time was discussed often on campus as indicated by the following posting from Kiyo Matsumoto.

> Two summers ago, my husband got into a bike accident. When I got to the hospital, his face was unrecognizable. When a doctor asked him if he could tell his name, the date and where we were, he stated his name, his

birthday and the place he used to live with his family. That time, I was in a major shock, but now thinking back the event, I find it very interesting. My husband, the doctor, the nurse, our friends and myself all physically existed in a same moment but my husband was not living on same timeline as rest of us lived. Even the 40 minutes I had to wait for our friends to come (never ending long one) must be different from their 40 minutes rushing to the hospital. (ties-edu.org/campus/HMC2 Bohm, Peat-Briggs integrative seminar, 1:75)

Another aspect of time was also discussed by Kiyo Matsumoto:

To be able to sense and see the moments of truth, once again, we would need adequate time and space to do it. We might be just too busy to have real dialogue in our life. Many of us feel and see the needs same way as Bohm suggests but yet we have not been able to act on them. It cannot be all this simple but if we can all slow down on our life, it might provide us opportunities to have true dialogue, which, I believe, will lead us to a peaceful world. (tiesedu.org/campus/HMC2 Bohm, Peat-Briggs integrative seminar, 1:76)

I enjoy the freedom that being in a Montessori classroom gives me to be able to have real dialogue with my students. The sense of connection that is felt when this is experienced makes all the long hours and low pay worth it. It is in those moments that I see eternity in the eyes of my students.

I have come to a point during this time in which I have repeatedly been impressed with the genius of the materials that Montessori created. I now trust that if I do a thorough job of explaining how to use the material, the student can then explore and discover their personal knowledge of the lesson we are working on. I understand this type of learning is not only more effective but it also increases the self esteem of the student in a way that traditional teaching never seemed to do.

I have been blessed during this journey to meet many new friends and co-workers that are all learning and sharing these same themes. These friendships have had a tremendous impact on my thoughts, dreams, and future plans. I see that meeting someone that is a Montessori teacher will imply to me a set of values, and a special way of looking at the world. It will connect me to them in a way that only many hours of study and soul searching can do. I will understand they probably also see that everything in our universe is interconnected and we all play a part.

I understand in a new way that everyone has a reason, a purpose, and something to share. For this reason I look deeper into the eyes of everybody I come into contact with and if they do not understand their purpose I try to honor them and create a space to help them to discover it.

Transformation has occurred in my life because I have taken the time to listen to my own thoughts and search for new ways when things don't seem to be working. This emphasis on looking within and dealing with the emotions discovered has led me to be a more conscientious person, and given me a deeper sense of inner peace. Looking within has encouraged me to base decisions in my life from a different perspective. Briggs and Peat describe it in this way:

> Perhaps for this reason many of the world's wisdom traditions teach that an action should not only take into account the welfare of others in the

future, it should be based on the authenticity of the moment, on being true to oneself, and exercising the values of compassion, love, and basic kindness. Positive butterfly power involves a recognition that each individual is an indivisible aspect of the whole and that each chaotic moment of the present is a mirror of the chaos of the future. Remember that Cezanne and Keats suggested that authentic truth is also rooted in a certain kind of attention to uncertainty and doubt. Positive butterfly power, which is really the power of the open system, comes from there. (Briggs & Peat, 2000, p. 42)

When I look at my Montessori experience as a whole, I recognize the process of observation, reflection, and always searching for ways to bring about gentleness and honor in each moment has had a butterfly effect in my own life. It has been a slow and emotionally challenging process, and while I do sometimes wonder what direction I will be taking in the future, it is lovely to know that my experience has forever changed me into a deeper and richer individual. For these reasons, I am very proud to now call myself, "A Montessori teacher."

Program Summary

Bifurcation point is a term which signifies a change in perspective or direction, similar to the point where a tree branches into a new direction. I have become intimately acquainted with this idea in the past few years since beginning the journey that would lead me from owning my own bookstore to going through an intensive training to gain my Montessori certification, onward towards a master's degree in Montessori integrative learning. Each new juncture has provided new growth and understanding of who I am as a person and the purpose of my journey through the world. As Wheatley describes, I have opened myself up to the unknown.

> Wouldn't we all welcome more playfulness in our lives? I would be excited to encounter people delighted by surprises instead of being scared to death of them.
>
> Were we to become truly good scientists of our leadership craft, we would seek out surprises, relishing the unpredictable when it finally decided to reveal itself. Surprise is the only route to discovery, a moment that pulsates with new learnings. The dance of this universe requires that we open ourselves to the unknown. Knowing the steps ahead of time is not important; being willing to engage with the music and move freely onto the dance floor is what's essential. (Wheatley, 1999, p. 162)

What I have discovered during this journey is that while I started looking for implications of peace within the Montessori environment, the more I opened myself up, the more I was able to find implications of peace everywhere I turned. Could it be possible as quantum theory suggests, I was co-creating peace in the world through my choice to observe peace in my environment?

Inner Peace

As I realized the need for a Montessori teacher to start with self I was indeed reaching deep within my own heart and actions to discover what it meant for me to choose to be peaceful. It occurred to me that if on a subatomic level the probability for more than one outcome could occur, then it could be possible in my life, that everyday, in every situation, the probability of peace could occur. I started looking for ways to actively seek out and make the choice for peace in my life. As I turned inward to search for answers I recognized how important respect was when making a choice for peace. I had to first respect myself. I had often heard the admonition of Jesus from Matthew 19:19 to love others as yourself. What challenges me is the truth that I have to see my own worth and love myself in order to care about and love others. In an online posting Julia Thiele reflected on her experience with this concept.

> My upbringing was to always respect another's thought to the point of putting my own down. It made me fit in Japan as an exchange student - people said I was "nihon teki" (like a Japanese). Part of this made me feel good inside, but I felt that little earnest voice saying - there's me in here...a voice I kept quiet until a few years back. (ties-edu.org/campus/HMC2 Bohm, Peat-Briggs integrative seminar, 1:81)

When something annoys me about someone else, I am learning to look deeper within myself to see where that same character trait is in me that I have not reached peace with. The sooner I honor the unlovable in myself, the sooner I am able to honor the people around me.

Another realization that occurred as I looked within was that often the root cause of unrest, or lack of inner peace, had to do with fear. Either fear of losing something I held precious or fear of not getting something I wanted. When peace became more important to me than holding onto my fears, I discovered it was much easier to let go and trust that life was working for my benefit. McFarland addresses this need to self actualize in her book for teachers, *Shining Through*.

> As we consciously take the time to experience the peace and tranquility of our Spirit, we will be filled with joy and guided in our actions. We will have the confidence to be vulnerable and the humility to continually remove that which is keeping us from achieving our potential. As we work sincerely to self-actualize, we will achieve increasingly high degrees of excellence and model this for the children and others. (McFarland, 1993, p. 27)

The search for inner peace led me to search many different types of world wisdom literature. Each of which seemed to point me in the same direction. There is a reason for me to be here; there are purposes, and plans for my life. Yet there is also paradox, because the harder I try to search for those purposes, the more they seem to elude me. It is only by being in a place of contentment do I come to find peace. Ruben Habito discusses the idea of looking within in his book, *Living Zen, Loving God*.

> The Buddhist tradition, in agreement with many other wisdom traditions, tells us that what we are looking for is not to be found by looking outside

> ourselves. Our yearning is not fulfilled in the satisfaction of a material want, in this or that pleasurable sensation, in this or that philosophical idea, however sublime, in this or that religious concept. What we are really seeking deep in our hearts cannot be found by looking "outside."
>
> (Habito, 2004, p.13)

The Christian version of this idea can be found in Luke 1:17 which gives an explanation of the kingdom of God being within. Jon Kabat-Zinn quotes Lao-Tzu from the Tao-te-Ching in his book, *Wherever You Go There You Are*.

> The Master sees things as they are,
>
> without trying to control them.
>
> She lets them go their own way,
>
> and resides at the center of the circle. (Kabat-Zinn, 1994, p.120)

It has become more important for me to know there is a reason than to discover the actual reason. Lisa Freeman makes an observation about a posting that Julia Thiele had made on campus regarding faith.

> Julia wrote, "Others like myself find immense peace and rest in a stage of not knowing but living by faith. Not peace in ignorance but just peace in knowing that what we know now, we only know in part and thus there is much that we do not know. "- I appreciate your honesty here - and I think that if the human race ever got to a place where all was "known" then where would we be? The spirit of the human race is that we are constantly in awe and desiring to know more. (ties-edu.org/campus/HMC2 Capra, Sahtouris, and Montessori, integrative seminar, 4:58)

Each time I try to reach out and control my destiny; my sense of peace gets distorted. It is always when I let go and trust that everything in the universe is unfolding as it should that my peace returns. It is the same in the classroom, the simple act of trusting and observing the classroom rather than trying to control outcomes is what ushers in a sense of peace. The very moment I try to force my ideas is the moment that negativity occurs.

I have discovered that not only do I need to come early to school in order to start the day with a moment of quiet reflection before students arrive, but I also that it is a good idea to eat my lunch by myself. This gives me a chance to breathe deeply and recharge my spirit before students return to the classroom. In a culture where everything seems to move quickly, I have noticed I have to make time for peace. I have not reached a point of peace being totally automatic. I have to create a space and a time to center my thoughts, a chance to recognize any areas for which I may need to make amends for and then do it quickly, so negative emotions do not have the opportunity to build up. I also need to reflect on positive experiences and use them to store up positive thoughts. Memories can be a beautiful example of the right use of imagination. When I am feeling stressed, recalling a memory of being at the beach during calm periods of my life is enough to help me overcome the anxiety of the moment.

When I was in training at the Houston Montessori Center the opportunity was presented for the trainees to be able to take a yoga class one day a week during our lunch break. I had never taken yoga before and found it to be a very restful way to allow my body a chance to release the stress that built up from the mental strain of class work. From this experience I learned the importance of taking even short breaks in order to rejuvenate my spirit. Often I will take a moment to get quiet and readjust my breathing rate before continuing an activity. This awareness of my breath relaxes me and reminds me of purpose outside of the moment that I am in. Sometimes this simple act of awareness is all that is needed to center my emotions and make a choice for peace.

In looking for ways to expand inner peace, I have noticed a need to not take my self too seriously. I find great humor in this thought from Macrina Wiederkehr's book, *A Tree Full of Angels,*

> There were evenings, too, when I stood in need of special protection. I would look out my window at that little sycamore in the moonlight, and I am next to sure its branches were full of angels. Heaven is like that. There will always be someone heaven-sent to "go out on the limb" for me until I am able to make the journey myself. Gazing at that tree full of angels, I began to realize that it wasn't because the tree was too little that I couldn't go on its limbs. It was because I am too heavy. Now I understand the meaning of the sign in my friend's kitchen that says, "Angels fly because they take themselves lightly." Perhaps leaves fly for the same reason. How hard it is to let go! (Wiederkehr, 1995, p. 134)

It has touched me that a sense of humor is a way of letting go of the stress of life and inviting in peace. My students love to laugh and love it when I join them in a good laugh. It is a reminder that life can be fun and adventurous. When things get a little too difficult and serious in our room, I try to find ways to bring in some joy and laughter. This might come in the form of a visiting pet, or a short game, or some type of surprise. This has been especially effective at times when there has been a major conflict that we are having a hard time getting through. When our class was trying to cope with the constant negative behavior of one student, I dyed my hair from its natural dirty blonde color to an intense shade of red. That may seem insignificant, after all people change their hair color all the time, but I knew the sensation it would cause in our classroom would give the students something enjoyable to discuss and joke with me about in order to distract them from the problem at hand.

I have discovered that sometimes stepping back and putting a problem into perspective gives an opportunity to see other options. Gaining a wider perspective not only helps to diminish a problem but it also lessens the emotional charge of a situation, which allows everyone involved the chance to regain a positive center to work from.

This same technique of widening the lens can apply to another aspect of inner peace, choosing an attitude of gratitude. Discovering the positive in any situation or person provides a sense of harmony, and opens up a willingness to work towards positive outcomes. One example of this is my attitude about grading papers. When I concentrate on the time and energy it may take to check math timed test I find myself becoming grumpy and losing all sense of inner peace. However, when I change my attitude and concentrate on assessments as a way to know my students and their needs better, I find my resentment and frustration slipping away.

As a part of my TIES experience I gave a presentation to an audience about the things I have learned since entering my training experience. I asked the audience members to think of practical ways that they could help create a peaceful world through three different ideas: inner peace, environmental peace, and peace within relationships.

The following ideas are some of their thoughts about creating inner peace.

- Be anxious for nothing.
- Keep peace in myself by seeking God's guidance each day.
- Stay in touch with my whole being instead of fragmented parts.
- Take time daily to reflect.
- Practice meditative readings of the gospels.
- Prayer
- Yoga practice and meditative time to focus on my place in the universe and the impact of nature on me
- To smile more, and love myself
- Turning the big and little things over to my higher power to solve
- I will remember that sometimes God calms the storm and sometimes God allows the storm to rage and calms His child.
- Face fear; know it will hurt, do it anyway
- Be patient with myself

Environmental Peace

Peace in the physical environment has played a very large part in the information I gained as a result of being a part of the TIES program. What I came to realize is that environmental peace has many different facets. When I make decisions for how to interact and care for the environment I am also making decisions about how to care and interact with the present and future inhabitants that share this planet.

Marilyn Waring in the book, *Counting for Nothing*, shares this thought about our world's water supply:

> Along with food, shelter, and clean air to breathe, nothing can be deemed to be more important to the "well-being of a community" than the supply of fresh water. While some water is now bottled and marketed, this amount is miniscule. Fresh water is absolutely necessary for the maintenance of life and health. Its nonavailability causes enormous sickness, disease, and death, not simply for human beings, but also for animal and plant life. The vast amounts of pollution vomited into our air, the raising of the earth's temperatures, the deforestation in many regions of the earth's temperatures, all lead to changes in the hydrological cycle.
> (Waring, 1999, p.208)

System theory reminds us that if there is a problem with the system, we need more information and awareness to build up and support the system. It also explains the process of caring for the system. Wheatley suggests to us, "If a system is in trouble, it can be restored to health by connecting it to more of itself. To make a system stronger, we need to create stronger relationships. (Wheatley, 1999, p.145) Montessori's ideas about giving the child a vision of the whole world in order to help discover their own sense of identity is also a way of seeing the unequivocal link each person has to the promotion or destruction of the environment. Capra expresses this idea of connectedness in *The Web of Life*,

> Deep Ecology recognizes the intrinsic value of all living beings and views humans as just one particular strand in the web of life.

> Ultimately, deep ecological awareness is spiritual or religious awareness. When the concept of the human spirit is understood as the mode of consciousness in which the individual feels a sense of belonging, of connectedness, to the cosmos as a whole, it becomes clear that ecological awareness is spiritual in its deepest essence. (Capra, 1996, p. 7)

These ideas have impacted me personally numerous ways. First of all, they have produced a greater awareness of world resources and the impact my use of these resources may have on the world. I have attempted to think through the things I purchase, the business practices of the stores at which I shop, the amount of packaging used, and the longevity of the objects I am purchasing. I have been inspired by my friend Warren Greene who firmly refuses to shop at any business that offers lower prices but engages in many unethical practices. As he has said, "Not all money is good money." This thought has caused me to understand that it is not worth me saving five dollars if someone else is worse off because of it.

Eighteen years ago I made the decision to become a vegetarian after reading Francis Lappe's book, *Diet For A Small Planet*. I made the decision because I was very concerned about how much water and grain goes into the raising of animals for a meat-based diet. For me the choice to do without meat in order that more of those resources would be available was a simple thing that I could do. However, since being a part of the TIES program and especially since reading *Next of Kin* by Roger Fouts, I have recognized that I have a deeper empathy for the animals that share our planet. It occurs to me that the wisdom that is within the child is also within the other creatures of our world that I have too quickly dismissed or ignored. This section of Fouts signifies that there may be many things we could learn by observing our animal neighbors closer.

> The peoples of West Africa, who have lived side by side with chimpanzees for aeons, have never thought of them as being deficient in their ability to reason. On the contrary, they have long known that chimpanzees make and use stone tools, medicate themselves with indigenous plants, organize social activities hunting, and even have a rudimentary form of political culture. (Fouts, 1997, p.48)

Fouts also shared stories about the compassion of animals including a story about his family dog, Brownie, which uncharacteristically started barking passionately and chasing the family truck in an effort to gain attention. Then without warning, she jumped in front of the truck sacrificing her own life in order to save Fout's brother, whom only she could see was stuck in a deep rut in the road and would have been hit by the truck in a few seconds. (Fouts, 1997, p.6)

Now that I have come to a greater understanding of the relevance of environmental peace I would like to find ways to raise the awareness of others around me. Julia Thiele shared her thoughts about ecoliteracy on campus:

> If we are to become ecoliterate, it does seem that starting with the young, through education is where we need to focus, but at the same time, the children alone can't be expected to carry this. Can we involve our families more in the active forming of networks, rather than them being on the periphery of what we are trying to achieve in our classrooms? Can we move beyond that into community? These are questions which come to

mind as I ponder ecoliterate education. (ties-edu.org/campus/HMC2,

Capra, Sahtouris, and Montessori, integrative seminar, 4:14)

Following are the choices of environmental peace that were shared by the community that I did my presentation for:

- Consider how my actions today affect others here and around the world.
- Buy used clothes.
- I will walk more-drive less.
- Pick up someone else's trash.
- Be a caretaker of the earth.
- Buy local things-exported items require gas waste and pollution from the shipping.
- Buy things with the least amount of packaging. For instance, if you want to buy a soda, don't get a six pack, get a 2 liter, even if you are going to recycle.
- Recycle more.
- Touch my body in some way to the earth each day. The helps me to remember that we are caretakers of the earth.
- Reduce waste
- Use what's available.
- Support eco-friendly businesses and farms.
- Buy less junk.
- Look into finding more organic food sources.

Marilyn Eblen, a mother of one of my students, shared a story about realizing that since the amount of trash around our school bothered her she could stop complaining, get out of her comfort zone, and pick it up. This idea that we can be a part of cleaning up the environment even when we were not the cause of the problem really resonated with me. I realized that the joy of doing something that would make the world cleaner and healthier was more than enough of a reason to do it.

Peace Within Relationships

Peace within relationships was the final idea that I asked my audience to consider as a way to create peace in the world. These are the choices they recognized they needed to implement or continue to do:

- Consider another perspective.
- Assume the best of others, even when they disappoint.
- Reach out to others, discover their needs.
- I will always assume that others have my best interests at heart.
- Be careful to save face for the bully and the victim.
- Have a calm, quiet voice.
- Treat others the way I want to be treated, but don't always expect to receive that in return. Be prepared to be lenient with other's attitudes.
- Choose to be happy.
- Remember that this person is a child of God, just like me.
- Use kind words.
- I will listen more, talk less.

Many of these ideas reflect to me the importance of honoring and respecting others. Through this process I have learned that my commitment to peace has come to the point that it is emotionally uncomfortable for me to deal with conflict in an unkind manner. I believe that it is possible to raise the consciousness of many others so that they feel the same way.

One person who worked during her lifetime to raise the consciousness of others was a woman that changed her name to Peace Pilgrim and walked across America. She walked 25,000 miles between the years 1953 through 1981 sharing her message of peace to those she came in contact with. Peace Pilgrim is a wonderful example of someone that at a very basic level made a decision to use what she had to reach out to others and share a message of inner and relationship peace. Currently another person who is trying to raise consciousness is Representative Dennis Kucinich of Ohio, who has introduced a Bill to create a Department of Peace. Commenting on the possible creation of a United States Department of Peace, Walter Cronkite is quoted on peacealliance.org as having this to say about conflict resolution.

> What is quite clear -- and would become clear as you go along with this campaign - is that you are trying, and I consider myself with you on this in every way... [To create] not only a massive but a basic change in our culture, in our entire approach to our relationships with other human beings... It's not a matter of simply getting another Department of government. You're speaking of an entire philosophical revolution.

It seems to me that for many reasons we have been conditioned over the years to choose either fight or flight as our only options for handling conflict, but now these options are not meeting our needs. There are many people who seem to be evolving in their desires and abilities to seek out other methods of conflict resolution. During her speech at the American Montessori Society annual conference in March 2006 in Houston, Texas, Wolf challenged members of The American Montessori Society to support the creation of a Department of Peace.

In his recent book, *Peace Is The Way*, Deepak Chopra shares similar thoughts to the ones that I first had as I first began this journey.

> The way of peace is based on the same thing that ushered in the age of science: a leap in consciousness. When they witnessed demonstrations of steam engines, electric lights, and vaccines, people adapted to them at the level of their awareness. The idea of being human could no longer be consistent with reading by candlelight, traveling by horse, suffering through high rates of death in childbirth, short life spans, and the ravages of disease. A leap in consciousness took place. The way of peace, I believe, can change the future in the same way. If you and I demonstrate that peace is more satisfying than war, the collective consciousness will shift. (Chopra, 2005, p.5)

Ideas about collective consciousness were discussed often on campus. Julia Thiele stated,

> Regarding the collective, I have always had a bit of trouble I understanding the value of collective prayer and this came up in a reading group lately, focused on a book called "Stalking Elijah" where the author was looking at Zen and other Eastern religions, and seeing where there

was a blending into the mystical side of Judaism. The rabbi leading the group began talking about the collective consciousness and how that was where communal prayer leads. For him there was value in individual and communal prayer, but that communal prayer has a different purpose and function in this way...and so perhaps can be more imbued with meaning. Reading the Seven lessons of chaos brought more understanding for me when listening to the rabbi talk. (ties-edu.org/campus/HMC2 Bohm, Peat-Briggs integrative seminar, 1:14)

I was brought to a point of questioning by the Briggs & Peat book *Seven Lessons of Chaos.*

> When Briggs says, "What attracts us to war?" I feel part of it is fear that there isn't enough and we have to steal or take from someone else in order to take care of ourselves. I see this in my work with married couples; there is such a fear that power will be taken away from one or the other until they finally realize that they are together on the same team and it is the team that needs to win and have power.
>
> My question is, how do we lift our collective conscious to bring the whole world onto the same team? (ties-edu.org/campus/HMC2 Bohm, Peat-Briggs integrative seminar, 1:16)

Gang in referring to my earlier posting:

> It seems to me that pushing for a change in consciousness regarding peace is a collaboration of the need for dialogue and a willingness to struggle through internal and external chaos in order to reach peace.

(ties-edu.org/campus/HMC2 Bohm, Peat-Briggs integrative seminar, 1:47)

As I have examined the many different aspects of the idea of peace, especially on a global perspective one of the things that I think would be very interesting would be if the entertainment media, specifically cinema, would take hold of the imaginative, limitless possibilities of peaceful conflict resolution. I wonder what would happen if theatrical role models were created who considered violence as juvenile and who instead strove to find original ways to solve problems. Already I have seen in the use of the Nobel Peace Prize material that I created for use in my classroom that students have been excited to choose people to study whom they had heard about the year before. They wanted to find out more about them. They are fascinated by the life stories of peacemakers who came from ordinary backgrounds but went on to lead unique lives because of their personal convictions and a desire to help the world. Peacemakers from other countries have generated a desire in my students to know about the cultures of those countries, thus inspiring a deeper respect for others who share our planet. I would love to create trading cards, similar to baseball trading cards, which are filled with the pictures and statistics of peacemakers of the world. It would be exciting to hear students discussing a trade of an Albert Schweitzer for a Betty Williams, and know that they knew who those people were and how they influenced the world.

As I leave this experience of the close online network which has been created through my Montessori training and my TIES coursework, it is a time of excitement to see what new adventures are waiting. Choosing peace is not always an easy option; it can be more challenging than using older, more familiar choices for solving conflicts. However, the more often the choice is made the easier it becomes. I am already looking forward to participating in several venues in order to share the information that I have learned about peace. One of these venues will be the opportunity to present a session in Washington, D.C. at the national conference of Phi Delta Kappa members next fall. Phi Delta Kappa is an honor society of teachers. I relish the thought of these teachers taking this information about peace back home with them and sharing them across the nation. When I first started to ask the question, "Do you think world peace is possible?" friends looked at me as if I had lost my mind. Here it is only a few years later and now those same friends are eager to hear about peace, and eager to start conversations about practical steps that they can take to walk on this journey of peace. Respected voices are starting to speak up and call for politicians to find new ways to solve political disputes in ways besides resulting to violence. I personally have become more involved at a grassroots level of political letter writing to both my congressional representatives and to the local editor of the newspaper to get across the idea that peace is a choice and the time to choose it is now.

As a teacher I realize every day how important my job is and that I am impacting the future through the students that I teach. Montessori was nominated several times for a Nobel Peace Prize for her beliefs that education could create an environment in which the spiritual growth of human could be fostered to such a point that war would no longer make sense. The examination of the Montessori environment has allowed me many opportunities to observe that her vision of a peaceful world has merit and is showing great progress. I have learned a great deal about inner peace for the transformation of myself as a teacher, about environmental peace for the protection and sustenance of the world around us, and about the importance of learning skills that foster relationships with others. It is my belief that the Montessori Method calls for a teacher who, through constant awareness and reflection, is able to create a safe and nurturing environment for the development of students. I believe that this method is a catalyst for lasting peace in the world.

Appendix

Peggy E. Pate-Smith

Research Proposal

Peace Education: Nobel Prize Winners

Introduction

When I was in the 6th grade I was inspired by a quote by the Roman philosopher, Seneca. The quote, "I would so live my life as if I received my being only for the benefit of others." took hold in my young heart and started a life long desire to live my life in such a way that I would not just be taking up space on this planet but actually be making a difference. That was also the same year that I decided that I wanted to be a teacher. One of the things that attracted me the most to Montessori education was the philosophy that the way to make the world a more peaceful place is through the education of the child. Recently I was able to attend a lecture given by Nobel Peace Prize winner, Jody Williams, where she challenged, "That if each one of us or even just handfuls found a way to make the world a better place, can you imagine the difference we would make." (Jody Williams, University of Tennessee at Martin, lecture, November 8, 2004)

Methodology

Louise Diamond states in the introduction of *The Peace Book*, "To live a culture of peace in the midst of war is an act of great simplicity, for you are proving that one person can make a difference." (Diamond, 2001, XIX) As children grow and develop I believe they seek out role models to help guide their way. My project is an effort to introduce students to positive role models that can inspire them. Specifically I plan to introduce students to winners of the Nobel Peace Prize through the use of stories, nomenclature, time lines, and research.

My desire is to learn what it is like for students to experience peace education through the tools created to teach them about Nobel Prize winners and how it may change their perspectives about the world. I would especially like to see if studying this topic brings them to a space where they could see themselves as being able to have a positive impact on the world. I am also interested in learning how studying this topic impacts the larger community. Will there be a greater interest in solving problems peacefully and will their families see any difference as a result of them experiencing these materials?

Methods

To accomplish this goal I will be incorporating a variety of methods. I will choose a specific group of students to create active interviews, meaning interviews with questions that are influenced and led by delving deeper into the experiences being explained by the person being interviewed. Active interviews are explained in the book, *Active Interview* by James Holstein, H and Jaber F. Gubrium (Holstein, and Gubrium, 1995). I will guide the interview using the following introductory questions:

When you learned about Nobel Prize winners, what were some ways that you saw that they made a difference in the world? Which of the winners impressed you the most and why? What do you think made these people do something special for the world around them? How has studying about Nobel Peace Prize winners helped you to see that even just one person can make a difference in the world? What are some ways that you feel that you might could change the world to make it a more peaceful place?

I will also be collecting their research to determine the things the children felt were important about various prize winners. The research form that students will use will include this format:

        Name of Nobel Prize winner:

        Birth date:

        Year of death:

        Year they won the Nobel Prize:

        Why they won the Nobel Prize:

When students share their research information I will be recording any dialogue that follows to enable me to gain insights about what they have learned and any new perspectives they may have gained as a result of learning about these Nobel Prize winners.

I also will be choosing specific parents to do active interviews with using the following questions:

We have been studying Nobel Peace Prize winners, what are some ways your child has brought this topic up at home? In what ways do you feel like studying this topic will be or has been beneficial to your child? Are there any ways that you have been impacted by your child's study of Nobel winners? Are there any ways that you personally try to make the world a more peaceful?

Hermeneutic

I will be using thematic analysis to bring meaning to the information and interviews that I collect. I will be using the three interpretive processes as suggested by Max Van Manen in his book, *Researching the Lived Experience*, (Van Manen, 1997/2003 p.92) to uncover themes that run consistently through my gathered information.

In using the wholistic approach I will try to distill the information into a phrase that contains the essence of that experience. I will then compare these phrases to create a common theme. The selective reading approach will be used as I pinpoint specific ideas that seem vital to the meaning of each experience being looked at. A detailed reading approach will allow me to examine each sentence in a research or interview to unlock crucial aspects of the experience that is described. The combination of these three approaches will allow me the opportunity to discover what it is like to experience peace education through the interaction with materials created specifically to learn more about Nobel Peace Prize winners.

References

Diamond, L. (2003) The Peace Book. Berkeley: Conari Press

Holstein, J. and Gubrium, J. (1995) *The Active Interview*. Thousand Oaks, CA: Sage Publications.

Van Manen, Max (1997/2003) *Researching The Lived Experience*. Toronto, Canada: The Althouse Press.

Williams, J. University of Tennessee at Martin, lecture on November 8, 2004.

References

Berry, T. (1999) *The Great Work.* New York, NY: Bell Tower.

Bealle, C. ties-edu.org/campus/HMC2 Swimme, Gang, integrative seminar, 3:10.

Bohm, D. (2003) *On Dialogue.* Nichol, L. (Ed.). Bodmin, Cornwall: MPG Books Ltd.

Briggs, J. & Peat, D. (2000) *Seven Lessons of Chaos.* New York, NY: HarperCollins Publishers.

Beudel, H. ties-edu.org/campus/HMC2 Bohm, Peat-Briggs integrative seminar, 1:117.

Beudel, H. ties-edu.org/campus/HMC2 Capra, Sahtouris, and Montessori, integrative seminar, 4:91.

Capra, F. (1997) *The Web of Life.* New York: Anchor Books.

Chase, C. (2001) *Madeline L' Engle Herself.* Colorado Springs, CO: WaterBrook Press.

Chattin-McNichols, J. (1998) *The Montessori Controversy.* Albany, NY: Delmar Publishers.

Chopra, D. (2005) *Peace Is the Way.* New York, NY: Harmony Books.

Crain, W. (1980/2000) *Theories of Development.* Upper Saddle River, NJ: Prentice Hall.

Cronkite, W. (2005) peacealliance.com.

Denomme, M. ties-edu.org/campus/HMC2, Bohm, Peat-Briggs integrative seminar, 1:1.

Dennison, G. & Dennison, P. (1994/1989) *Brain Gym.* Ventura, CA: The Educational Kinesiology Foundation.

Diamond, L. (2001) *The Peace Book.* Berkeley, CA: Conari Press.

Duffy, Michael & D'Neil (2002) *Children of the Universe.* Hollidaysburg, PA: Parent Child Press.

Ehrmann, M. (1979) *The Desiderata of Happiness.* (6th ed.) Boulder, CO: Blue

Mountain Press.

Emoto, M. (2004) *The Hidden Messages in Water.* Hillsboro, OR: Beyond Words Publishing.

Freeman, L. ties-edu.org/campus/HMC2 Capra, Sahtouris, and Montessori, integrative seminar, 4:58.

Fouts, R. (1997) Next *of Kin.* New York, NY: William Morrow and Company, Inc.

Gang, M. ties-edu.org/campus/HMC2 Bohm, Peat-Briggs integrative seminar, 1:47.

Gang, P. & Morgan, M. (DVD) (2003) *Introduction to Montessori Radical Education.* Christchurch, NZ: The Institute for Educational Studies.

Gang, P. (1989) *Rethinking Education.* Christchurch, NZ: Degaz Press.

Gibran, K. (1923/1982*) The Prophet.* New York, NY: Random House.

Goertz, D. (2001) *Children Who Are Not Yet Peaceful.* Berkeley, CA: Frog, Ltd.

Grazzini, C. (1996) *The Four Planes of Development.* The NAMTA Journal, Volume 21, No.2, p.223.

Jensen, E. (1998). *Teaching with the Brain in Mind.* Alexandra, VA: Association for Supervision and Curriculum Development.

Kabat-Zinn, J. (1994) *Wherever You Go, There You Are*. New York, NY: Hyperion.

Habito, R. (2004*) Living Zen, Loving God*. Somerville, MA: Wisdom Publications.

Holstein, J. and Gubrium, J. (1995) *The Active Interview.* Thousand Oaks, CA: Sage Publications.

Krishnamurti, J. (1981) *Education and the Significance of Life.* New York, NY: Harper and Row.

Lappe, F. (1971/1991) *Diet for a Small Planet*. New York, NY: Random House.

Mitsumoto, K. ties-edu.org/campus/HMC2 Bohm, Peat-Briggs integrative seminar, 1:7)

Matsumoto, K. ties-edu.org/campus/HMC2 Bohm, Peat-Briggs integrative seminar, 1:75)

Matsumoto, K. ties-edu.org/campus/HMC2 Bohm, Peat-Briggs integrative seminar, 1:75.

Matsumoto, K. ties-edu.org/campus/HMC2 Capra, Sahtouris, & Montessori, integrative seminar, 4:86.

Matulli, A. ties-edu.org/campus/HMC2 Bohm, Peat-Briggs integrative seminar, 1:58.

McAvey, V. ties-edu.org/campus/HMC2 Swimme, Gang, integrative seminar, 3:73.

McFarland, S. (1993) *Shining Through, A Teacher's Handbook on Transformation.* Denver, CO: Shining Mountains Center.

Montessori, M. (1912/2002) *Discovery of the Child.* Oxford, Eng.: Clio Press.

Montessori, M. (1949/1992) *Education and Peace.* Oxford, England: Clio Press.

Montessori, M. (1948/2002) *To Educate the Human Potential.* Oxford, England: Clio Press.

Morris, W. (1969/1975) *The American Heritage Dictionary.* New York, NY: American Heritage Publishing Co.

Nhat Hanh, T. (1987) *Being Peace.* Berkeley: CA: Parallax Press.

Pearson, D. ties-edu.org/campus/HMC2 Capra, Sahtouris, and Montessori, integrative seminar, 4:27.

Reynolds, D. (1997/2002) *A Handbook for Constructive Living*. Honolulu, Hawaii: Kolouala Books: University of Hawaii Press.

Smith, P. ties-edu.org/campus/HMC2 Bohm, Peat-Briggs integrative seminar, 1:16)

Smith, P. ties-edu.org/campus/HMC2 Swimme, Gang, integrative seminar, 3:89.

Sahtouris, E. (2000) *EarthDance*. Lincoln, NE: University Press.

Stiekel, B. (2005) *The Nobel Book of Answers*. New York, NY: Simon & Schuster, Inc.

Swimme, B. (1996) *The Hidden Heart of the Cosmos*. Maryknoll, NY: Oribis Books

Thiele, J. ties-edu.org/campus/HMC2 Bohm, Peat-Briggs integrative seminar, 1:3.

Thiele, J. ties-edu.org/campus/HMC2 Bohm, Peat-Briggs integrative seminar, 1:81.

Thiele, J. ties-edu.org/campus/HMC2 Capra, Sahtouris, and Montessori, integrative seminar, 4:14.

Van Manen, M. (1997/2003) *Researching The Lived Experience*. Toronto, Canada: The Althouse Press.

Waring, M. (1999) *Counting for Nothing: What Men Value, What Women Are Worth*. Toronto, Canada: University of Toronto Press.

Wheatley, M. (1999). *Leadership and the New Science*. San Francisco, CA: Berrett Koehler Publishers Inc.

Wiederkehr, M. (1990) *A Tree Full of Angels*. San Francisco, CA: Harper Collins.

Williams, R. ties-edu.org/campus/HMC2 Bohm, Peat-Briggs integrative seminar, 1:81.

Wink, W. (2003) *Jesus and Nonviolence*. Minneapolis, MN: Fortress Press.

Wolf, A. (1996) *Nurturing the Spirit*. Pennsylvania, PA: Parent Child Press.

www.ingramcontent.com/pod-product-compliance
Lightning Source LLC
Chambersburg PA
CBHW071124090426
42736CB00012B/2002